MW00934563

THE PRAYER BOX

The Power of
Spiritual Discipline

Paula Bryant-Ellis

THE PRAYER BOX

The Power of Spiritual Discipline

Paula Bryant-Ellis
Mary Esther Ruth
6230 Wilshire Blvd. #895
Los Ángeles, CA 90048-5126
Email: **maryestherruthblog@gmail.com**
Website: **maryestherruth.com**

Copyright © 2018 by Paula Bryant-Ellis
All rights reserved.
Printed in the United States of America

ISBN-10: 1725860090
ISBN-13: 978-1725860094
BISAC: Religion/Prayer

> *"PRAYER IS THE KEY OF THE MORNING AND THE BOLT IN THE EVENING"*

MAHATMA GANDHI

DEDICATION

To my mother, you gave me the GIFT OF LIFE, thank you! I pray and war for you daily. I love you!

~

To my husband, you are a gift from heaven! I am so honored to be your wife. YOU BELIEVED IN ME, AND YOUR LOVE FOREVER CHANGED ME! I pray and war for you daily. I love you, husband! Wife-4-Life.

~

To my son, YOU'VE INSPIRED ME TO DREAM AGAIN! I'm so honored that God allowed me to be your mother. I still can't believe He wanted a part of me as a part of you. I pray and war for you daily my son. You are a blessing from heaven. I love you!

~

To my family (step-father, two sisters, many nieces and nephews, great niece and nephew, mother-in-law and brothers-in-law), I love you ALL! I pray and war for you daily.

~

To Jesus Christ, who sacrificed His life and put His name on every petition that was and that will come FOREVER. You are my Savior, and I love you! I AM A BELIEVER, I AM A FOLLOWER, AND I AM A WORSHIPER IN SPIRIT AND IN TRUTH.

CONTENTS

YOU'RE A SOLDIER FOR THE KINGDOM

I'm so humbled that you've decided to purchase THE PRAYER BOX. I'm excited that you've made the commitment to do the work that it takes to enrich your prayer life. There's nothing more important than your relationship with Christ. The only way to diligently seek Him is to spend time in His Presence. How can you build a relationship with someone, if you don't spend time with that person?

Think about your most trusted, personal relationship today. It could be a spouse, family member or friend. Intimacy and trust happens because you've spent time together. You've endured trials together. You trust one another. You're comfortable in their presence, and you trust their judgment. They've revealed themselves to you, and you've revealed yourself to them. You can count on them, and they can count on you through thick and thin. Your commitment to the relationship helped build what you have today. Every meaningful relationship requires an investment of our personal time. Well, it is the same with God.

Let me be clear; you don't need anything in this box to enrich your prayer life with God. If you have the discipline, you can do it on your own. But today you decided to buy the prayer box. You've decided to commitment to the hard work. You've decided to invest in your prayer life because you want a relationship with Christ. You want something deeper than what you have right now. Trust me; I completely understand how you feel because I've been there myself. There are no gimmicks here. There is no quick fast way to develop a relationship with God. Let me assure you; any meaningful relationship, requires sacrifice, trust, commitment and time.

Did you know that as you build your relationship with Christ, you also develop as a spiritual warrior? Make no mistake about it; **YOU ARE AT WAR!** Every day that you walk this earth, you're living in a war zone and the enemy seeks to engage you by any means necessary.

> *Be sober, be vigilant; because your adversary the devil, as [he's not a lion, but he will sure try to make you think he's one] a roaring lion, walketh about, seeking whom he may devour [remember he needs your permission to devour you] (1 Peter 5:8, with my additional comments).*

When you enlist as a soldier in the military you're put through intense military training. Your training can last for six to thirteen weeks. This training is often referred to as Basic Training or Boot Camp. My father, stepfather, father-in-law and husband all served in the military. So I've heard many stories about the challenges you must endure during training.

Basic Training builds soldiers. That's its sole purpose. It builds top-notch, disciplined soldiers. A soldier capable of defending his/her country. You're taught survival skills as well as strategic tactics. These strategies prepare your mind for the mental games the enemy will try to use to attack you and to break you. Developing as a spiritual warrior is a lot like developing as a soldier. Both require mental discipline when engaging with the enemy.

> *For though we walk in the flesh, we do not war after the flesh: (For the weapons of our warfare are not carnal, but mighty through God to the pulling down of strong holds;) Casting down imaginations, and every high thing that exalteth itself against the knowledge of God, and bringing into captivity every thought to the obedience of Christ (2 Corinthians 10:3-5).*

Now, that right there is a mind game. *"Casting down imaginations, and every high thing that exalteth itself against the knowledge of God, and bringing into captivity every thought to the obedience of Christ."* Only those strong enough to surrender to the Will of God will endure the mental strategies of the enemy.

If you can imagine it, you can become it, that's the power of imagination. This is why the Bible tells you to cast down anything that comes up against what God says about you. If you imagine defeat, then you'll be defeated. If you imagine victory, then you'll have victory. Soldiers envision victory and complete annihilation of their enemy. This is what they've been trained to do.

Basic training teaches you to stop thinking like a civilian and start thinking as a soldier. Soldiers live with the constant threat of war. They keep their standard military gear packed and ready at all times. Even on their day off, they're ready for deployment. Their standard military gear includes the essentials needed for combat. It includes uniforms, boots, weapons, ammunition, and anything else needed for war. It's the same in spiritual warfare.

Prayer warriors live with the constant threat of spiritual warfare. Much like a soldier you have no days off. You must be ready for the tactics of the enemy at all times. When we pray without ceasing, we create a constant state of readiness. Prayer teaches you to stop thinking as an earthly civilian. It trains you to think as a spiritual warrior and to war in your original state of supernatural.

THE PRAYER BOX is like your standard military gear. It contains the essentials needed to prepare you for spiritual war. This box was curated to help you train and become a top-notch, disciplined soldier. Add your Bible and you're ready for basic training.

The prayer guide is not your traditional book on prayer. There are thousands of books that teach you how to pray. Few focus on the importance of developing spiritual disciplines. This guide is short and to the point. My intention is to get you on your knees as soon as possible. The time spent reading this book is time away from the Holy Spirit. The sooner you're on your knees praying, the sooner you'll start building a relationship with the Holy Spirit. It will be the most rewarding relationship you've ever encountered.

This prayer guide is the first in a three-part series. In it, you'll focus on developing a disciplined and consistent pattern of prayer. Prayer requires active participation. You must show up and engage in the process. My goal is to help you build an atmosphere of prayer as Jesus did. It will put you on a journey to enriching your relationship with Christ. You will be a soldier for the Kingdom.

CHAPTER 1

PURPOSE OF PRAYER

PRAYER IS COMMUNICATION

Before you get started using the essential items in your prayer box, it's important that we are in agreement on the purpose of prayer. But before we can discuss the purpose of prayer, we must agree on the definition of prayer.

What is Prayer?

So, what is prayer? Prayer is communication with God. It's that simple. It's our way of talking to Him and making our request known (Philippians. 4:6-7). Prayer is our most vital resource. We need prayer all the time (Luke 18:1). Unfortunately, most people will use prayer as a last resort rather than developing and understanding the magnificent gift of a powerful and effective prayer life.

In any close relationship, there has to be a two-way dialog. The strongest relationships have individuals who focus more on listening versus talking. They're focused on what's said as well as what's not being said. They're willing to tune their ears and not their lips. That's God. He allows us to come to Him with what's on our hearts, and He listens, but prayer is one way. It's one part of the communication process with God. Developing consistent prayer habits are essential to building a relationship with Christ. Once you've established a consistent foundation of prayer, you've opened your heart to hear the Voice of God.

Prayer is more than requesting help in time of need or desire. The dynamics of prayer are multi-dimensional. It can only be understood through time and experience. If you don't develop spiritual disciplines, you'll always be struggling in your prayer life.

Prayer Is a Supernatural Communication

Before Adam was kicked out of the Garden of Eden, he had full access to God. He had a relationship with the Creator. The second chapter of Genesis says,

> *And the Lord God took the man, and put him into the Garden of Eden to dress it and to keep it. And the Lord God commanded the man, saying, Of every tree of the garden thou mayest freely eat: But of the tree of the knowledge of good and evil, thou shalt not eat of it: for in the day that thou eatest thereof thou shalt surely die. And the Lord God said, It is not good that the man should be alone; I will make him an help meet for him. And out of the ground the Lord God formed every beast of the field, and every fowl of the air; and brought them unto Adam to see what he would call them: and whatsoever Adam called every living creature, that was the name thereof (Genesis 2:15-19).*

He was walking and talking with not just the Creator but with Creation. WOW! Did you catch that revelation? If God is the Creator, then He is the Creation. Can you imagine walking in the garden every day with God? Adam had supernatural communication with The Trinity (Father, Son and Holy Spirit).

In fact, Adam's original state was naturally supernatural. Imagine Adam had no idea what he was about to lose. All he'd ever known, at that time, was walking and talking with God. The supernatural was Adam's normal or original state.

Don't get all wired on me about the term supernatural. Supernatural is simply a force beyond scientific understanding. Isn't that God? He surpasses all scientific laws and understanding. That's supernatural. If you believe in God and that He created Adam, then you believe there was a force that they both existed in, that is beyond what we know today.

I love the fact that God actually "brought" the animals to Adam. God was working on Adam's behalf. Just think about their relationship. God came down from heaven and actually gave Adam a special assignment. Read verse 19, again.

> *And out of the ground the Lord God formed every beast of the field, and every fowl of the air; and brought them unto Adam to see what he would call them: and whatsoever Adam called every living creature, that was the name thereof.*

So Adam talked to God, received instructions from God, and he received assignments from Him as well.

I've often wondered, what had to be going through Adam's mind when he was chased out of the garden? Kicked out by God, no more supernatural communications, instructions or heavenly assignments. One minute, you're walking and talking with God and the next minute, you're out in the desert.

We've all been there; we've experienced something that's been abruptly taken away from us. It could have been the death of a loved one, the loss of a close friendship, the loss of a job or even the loss of your health. When it happened, it knocked you off your feet. You completely lost your bearings, and it happened in a split second.

Prayer takes us back to our original state of supernatural communications with God. It's meant to reconnect us to what was so abruptly taken away that day in the garden.

Prayer Influences

Does prayer influence God? Yes! One of my favorite stories in the Bible is about King Hezekiah.

> *In those days was Hezekiah sick unto death. And Isaiah the prophet the son of Amoz came unto him, and said unto him, Thus saith the Lord, Set thine house in order: for thou shalt die, and not live. Then Hezekiah turned his face toward the wall, and prayed unto the Lord, And said, Remember now, O Lord, I beseech thee, how I have walked before thee in truth and with a perfect heart, and have done that which is good in thy sight. And Hezekiah wept sore. Then came the word of the Lord to Isaiah, saying, Go, and say to Hezekiah, Thus saith the Lord, the God of David thy father, I have heard thy prayer, I have seen thy tears: behold, I will add unto thy days fifteen years. And I will deliver thee and this city out of the hand of the king of Assyria: and I will defend this city (Isaiah 38:1-6).*

First, we know that King Hezekiah was deathly ill. We also know that Isaiah has special instructions from God, for Hezekiah. He's told to set his house in order. WOW! But Hezekiah did something remarkable. He *"turned his face toward the wall and prayed unto the Lord."* As he was praying, he reminded God that he'd done what God had called him to do. Hezekiah said, *"I have walked before thee in truth and with a PERFECT heart and have done that which is good in thy sight."*

How many people can pray that prayer? How many people can stand before the Lord and say, *"I have a perfect heart?"* Now that's powerful! God told Isaiah to go back and tell Hezekiah that he heard him. God said he would add fifteen more years to his life and he would save him and his city from their enemy. Now, that's influence!

So, we've seen a couple of things here in this story. God gave specific instructions to Isaiah for Hezekiah. God was moved by King Hezekiah's deeds and influenced by his prayers.

Prayer is a Weapon

Prayer is the most potent weapon in our spiritual warfare. Imagine if our country was at war and the President had no way to communicate with his commanders in the field? He'd have no way to give them the information they need to protect our country. He'd have no way to let them know the strategic positions of troops in the field. They would not know how to locate food, water, medical supplies, weapons or ammunition. They would be defenseless against their enemy.

Well, if you don't pray daily, then that's exactly what happens to you. You're defenseless against the enemy, and you have left your loved ones exposed as well. Prayer is not only for you. It's also meant to protect your family, friends and anyone that you're responsible for covering. We have souls that we're responsible for covering in prayer. When we don't pray for them, they're left exposed to the tricks of the enemy.

First Thessalonians 5:17 says, *"Pray without ceasing."* Now, I don't (and I hope you don't either) believe this means to never stop praying. I do believe that it means we should maintain an atmosphere of prayer. Like a soldier, we need to be ready for war at all times.

Jesus maintained an atmosphere of prayer wherever he went. His life's journey remains a perfect reflection of that work. He prayed, whether he was alone or with friends. He prayed before important decisions. He prayed in public, before meals and before and after healing someone. That's praying without ceasing. He was always in a state of supernatural, ready to consult the Father at any time. Just think, Jesus was The Word and yet he still had to pray. My goodness, I hope you caught that; it's thought provoking and life changing. That simple statement alone should tell you how important prayer is in our lives. The Word had to pray. WOW!

Jesus made sure the disciples knew how to pray. Like any great General, he left behind a strategy for us to follow. He wanted to ensure we could communicate with him while we were away on assignment.

> *After this manner therefore pray ye: Our Father which art in heaven, Hallowed be thy name. Thy kingdom come, Thy will be done in earth, as it is in heaven. Give us this day our daily bread. And forgive us our debts, as we forgive our debtors. And lead us not into temptation, but deliver us from evil: For thine is the kingdom and the power, and the glory, forever. Amen (Matthew 6:9-13).*

I love the Lord's Prayer. Jesus gives us such insight about our responsibility and our relationship with the Father.

Our Father. Our Father, Abba; we can invoke, call upon, trust and believe in God. Revealed to us as Father by His son (John 1:18), He is loving, compassionate and the giver of life. He protects and takes care of His children.

In the New Testament, Jesus and Paul both addressed God as Abba. Abba is an Aramaic word that means father (daddy). It helps us to understand the level of personal intimacy God wants with His children. It also reveals that He wants us to have childlike trust with our Father. Abba is the blueprint for all fathers to follow. He is the King of kings and the Father of fathers.

Who art in heaven. Does God actually live in Heaven? Wouldn't that be limiting God? We would be putting borders around a God that has no boundaries. The phrase "who art in heaven" isn't a reference of a place or space, its referencing God as the creation.

> *Job 11:8-9 says, "It is as high as heaven; what canst thou do? deeper than hell; what canst thou know? The measure thereof is longer than the earth, and broader than the sea."*

God is Heaven. How do we know that? Because we know He is the Creator. We know He is the Creation itself because it all came from Him. So if He is Creation, then He is Heaven. There isn't any one place that could ever contain all that God Is. Heaven is where ever God is and He lives in you.

Hallowed be thy name. When we say, "hallowed be thy name", we are honoring God's name as Holy. We should be in awe and in reverence of who He is and what He's done. We have a responsibility to keep his name holy and sacred. What are you doing to keep the name of God sacred?

Thy kingdom come. We're asking that God's Kingdom of mercy, grace and love cover us here on earth. Jesus never instructed the disciples to pray that one day they would go to heaven. He instructed them to pray that God's Kingdom come to us here on earth. That His Kingdom meet us right here, in the now. Isn't that amazing? You do not have to die to experience the Kingdom of Heaven.

Thy will be done in earth as it is in heaven. Jesus asked the Father for two things. First, His will be done, and second that it be done "in earth" exactly as it is "in heaven." He was telling us to align with our Father's perfect will. By doing so, we give God permission to reign over our lives.

Give us this day our daily bread. The Bible as well as the Lord's Prayer makes it clear that God is in the present moment. He's a right now God. He never lives in the past, and the future is His to bless as He pleases. In this petition we're asking God to give us what we need for today, and that we trust Him to take care of tomorrow.

Forgive us our trespasses, as we forgive those who trespass against us. If you want to be forgiven you must be willing to forgive. It's that simple. Mark 11:25 says, *"And when you stand praying, if you hold anything against anyone, forgive him, so that your Father in heaven may forgive you your sins."* How can you expect God to show you mercy if you aren't willing to show mercy towards others? You're forgiven as much as you're willing to forgive.

Lead us not into temptation. We're asking God to give us the strength to withstand the temptations and dangers we face. James 1:12 says, *"Blessed is the man that endures temptation; for when he hath been proved he shall receive the crown of life, which God promised to them that love him."*

But deliver us from evil. We all know what it's like to face an enemy. Remember we are at war! We are being hunted for our eternity. I love that Jesus made sure we knew that God is our Deliverer. I know there have been times when you thought you'd never find your way out of a situation. Some of you might be there right now. But you can be confident in your prayers that He'll deliver you out of that situation. It may not look the way you thought it would, but He is a Deliverer!

The Bible tells us that when we've done all we can do to stand, **STAND**. God has already prevailed. Victory over evil was won the moment Jesus freely gave himself up to death so that He could give us life. Although, the earth is still in battle the war has already been won.

For thine is the kingdom, the power, and glory forever. Early manuscripts of Matthew don't contain this phrase. Known as the final doxology, it's a formula of praise to God. We end with a final "Amen". Amen means, "so be it". When we end our prayer with Amen we are giving our formal consent. We are in complete agreement with everything Jesus taught us in this prayer.

We should say the Lord's Prayer every day. Every day we need God's help to make it. We cannot do it alone. It was never meant for us to be without God. Whenever we say the Lord's Prayer we should always say it with reverential attention, because we received this prayer from Jesus Christ. The Lord's Prayer didn't come from a friend it came from the Word of God.

Jesus used prayer as a weapon. We've seen how he demonstrated an atmosphere of prayer every day. He prayed before eating (he fed the hungry), he prayed before healing (he healed the sick), and he prayed before major decisions (he saved souls, casted out demons and raised the dead). We are to do the same.

Prayer is Boldness

We must be willing to communicate with God with boldness. He's not offended by it at all because He created you in His image, so He expects it. He's a bold God and we are His bold children. When we go to God boldly, it builds our faith.

And this is the confidence that we have in him, that, if we ask anything according to his will, he heareth us: And if we know that he hear us, whatsoever we ask, we know that we have the petitions that we desired of him (1 John 5:14-15).

God loves when we have our facts straight about His Word. He delights when we come claiming what's ours just like Hezekiah did.

Put me in remembrance: let us plead together: declare thou, that thou mayest be justified (Isaiah 43:26).

Hezekiah knew that his heart was pure. He may have turned his face to the wall to pray, but to say "my heart is pure" that's boldness!

SUMMARY

So are we in agreement on the definition and purpose of prayer? Prayer is communication, and it's how we talk to God. Prayer is supernatural communication. It's how we receive special instructions and our daily assignments. Prayer is influential. We've seen God change a decision He'd previously made and had already communicated, through prayer. Prayer is a weapon, and the only way we can fight in spiritual warfare is through prayer. We're to be bold in prayer. We're to come confidently to the Father and put Him in remembrance of His Word.

So now that we're in agreement, we're ready to walk through the essential items in your prayer box. Get ready for Basic Training!

CHAPTER 2

THE PRAYER BOX ESSENTIALS

One day, a few months ago, I was praying about my journey. I was so appreciative and humble of my growth in the Word of God. While meditating later that day, I asked the Holy Spirit, "Why there wasn't a basic training kit for someone who'd accepted Jesus Christ as their Lord and Savior?" I said, "It could also help someone who wanted to grow and have a deeper, richer relationship with Him?" I sure could have used one on my journey. I started laughing, and I heard the Holy Spirit say, "Create one!"

I remember being age 16 and having no idea what to do next after I'd accepted Christ into my life. I was so young and innocent. I hadn't seen or experienced much. I was stuck in a place of depression and loneliness after my parents' divorce (I was age 13 then). Three years later, nothing much had changed for me. The pain was so heavy. What in the world do you do with all of that pain?

I adored my father but my mother moved us from Austin, Texas to Sacramento, California. I wouldn't see him again until I was twenty three years old. By then the wounds were deep.

Growing up, I attended a popular church. Every one dressed in the latest fashions every Sunday and they always drove the latest cars. There was so much gossiping and backstabbing going on in that church, it was unreal. It made me realize at a very young age that I didn't want religion. I was desperate for a relationship, even though I did not fully understand.

We had the best gospel choir in the city though! I was a member of the choir. I was so broken on the inside that I'd sit in the choir stand and cry every Sunday. No one had any idea of the dark things I'd contemplated trying to set myself free. No one ever gave me a scripture to meditate on or ever prayed for me. But we'd sing our hearts out until the same old folks would run down the aisle dancing and shouting. At age 16, I'd accepted Christ. It would be years before I would actually pick up a Bible and start reading. It would be years before I'd pray. I tell you, I could have really used a prayer box back then!

This box is curated for you with direction from the Holy Spirit. There are a lot of prayers and tears poured into this box. I've prayed over it, my husband has prayed over it and I've had other ministers and pastors prayed over it as well. Although I'm sharing some of the things I've used on my journey, I didn't want to do anything that is outside of the Will of God for you. In this box, you'll find the basic things you'll need to help you focus and build a life of spiritual discipline. With these items you'll find your own special way to connect with the Holy Spirit.

As you build discipline, you'll begin to build consistency. Once consistency is established you'll find relationship. This is not a box of uniformity. This is not a box of thoughtless routine. That's not the purpose of this prayer box. Everyone needs to establish his or her unique relationship with Christ. In this box, you'll find a few things I've used personally over the years and they've changed my life.

THE PRAYER PILLOW

There are several different positions of prayer. Did you know that your posture expresses your heart and attitude towards God? All throughout the Bible, we've read about different postures of prayer. In the Old Testament, we've read where Abraham fell on his face in the Presence of God. Moses stretched out his hands before God and King Hezekiah turned his face to the wall. In the New Testament, Jesus kneeled looking up to the heavens when he prayed. You can lie prostrate, kneel, bow, stand, sit or raise your hands while in prayer. If you have an active prayer life, you'll use each one at one time or another.

Over the years, I've used several different postures of prayer. Two years ago, I was diagnosed with ischemic optic neuropathy, an eye disease that causes complete blindness. When I came home that afternoon from my doctor's appointment, I laid out prostrate on my face. I told the Holy Spirit that I didn't believe that this was the journey he had for me. I did not believe He'd moved us to Los Angeles, had me quit my job to sit in complete darkness. But I said if it was, it didn't matter because I was going to trust Him and follow Him regardless.

When I meditate, I'm often in a sitting position. I like to sit in my favorite chair, during the early morning dawn with my window open and listen to the Holy Spirit. I sit in complete darkness because the light of the Holy Spirit is all I need to guide me.

But my favorite position of prayer is kneeling which is why I want to share this prayer pillow with you. I'll be honest, my prayer pillow has gotten pretty nasty over the years, and I'm not ashamed to admit it. It's been through some battles. It's been kneeled on, cried on, drooled on, sat on, balled up, folded up and even slept on. If this pillow could talk, it could tell all of my secrets. It knows every tear I've cried and every word that I've shared with the Holy Spirit.

Kneeling is a sign of reverence for a King, and it's common in both the Old and New Testaments. Kneeling is a sign of submission to God's power and authority. When we kneel before God, we are appealing to the King of kings. When we repent for our sins, we need His mercy (to hold back all of the things we deserve because of our sinful ways). We also need His grace (which blesses us even when we don't deserve it). I'm pretty sure that's something we should be doing on our knees. Philippians 2:9-11 says,

> *Wherefore God also hath highly exalted him, and given him a name which is above every name: That at the name of Jesus every knee should bow, of things in heaven, and things in earth, and things under the earth; And that every tongue should confess that Jesus Christ is Lord, to the glory of God the Father.*

I've never read anywhere in the Bible where a certain position is required to have a relationship with God. The disciples found Jesus in the garden on his knees praying, you can't go wrong by modeling his example. After all, he is the Word.

THE PRAYER GUIDE

This book that's in your hands right now is your prayer guide. It's meant to guide you through the steps I've taken over the years to develop my prayer life. As I said earlier in this book, nothing in this box is required for you to have a relationship with Christ. I'm sharing these items with you because they're special to me. Through my own personal journey, they've been the staples that I've leaned on over and over again.

Also this guide has 30 daily exercises to help you build spiritual discipline in your prayer life. The purpose of this box and these exercises are to help you form a habit of prayer. If you miss a day or two do not quit or feel defeated! Just pick up where you left off.

These exercises are meant to start you on a journey of building a relationship with the Holy Spirit. Struggling is just part of the process because there is no way the enemy wants you to have a relationship with Christ.

THE JOURNAL & WRITING PENS

It's so important to learn the exercise of journaling. It was life changing for me once I put it into practice. There have been times when I couldn't utter a single word in prayer, but I was able to write. So I began writing down my prayers and reading them aloud to the Holy Spirit. When you are in a dry or difficult place, it really works. It also helped me bring clarity and focus to my request.

I keep my prayer journals. I've been collecting them for about 15 years now. One of my favorite things to do is to go back and read what I wrote about in those old journals. I find untold peace when I read them. I find strength when I look back and see what God has brought me through. They've shown me how God kept His promises or He redirected me to something even greater than I imagined. Our God is in the prayer answering business. That's what He does. My journals serve as a reminder of God's mercy and grace in my life.

When you write in your prayer journal, remember to write your prayers down with your black ink pen. When you receive direction and revelation from the Holy Spirit, write it down with your red ink pen. That's the purpose of the two pens. When you pray, don't hesitate to read back to the Holy Spirit what you've written in your journal. Bring God's Word back to remembrance to Him, just like He told us to do.

COMMUNION

Jesus gave the disciples clear instructions on communion. Yet many Believers do not take communion at all. Luke 22:19-20 says,

And he took bread, and gave thanks, and broke it, and gave unto them, saying, This is my body, which is given for you: do this in remembrance of me. Likewise also the cup after supper, saying, This cup is the new testament in my blood, which is shed for you.

As clear as he was about taking communion, Jesus gave no directions or instructions on the frequency in which to take it. This leads me to believe that you can take it as often as your heart desires. First Corinthians 11:26 says,

For as often as you eat this bread and drink this cup, you proclaim the Lord's death until he returns.

It's a sacrifice to take communion. It requires a lot of self-reflection. I don't want to take it if my heart does not have the right posture and attitude towards anyone in my life. I want my will to surrender completely to His Will. I want my heart to be clean and washed by the Spirit of the Word. I want to be a better daughter, wife, mother, sister, aunt, and niece. I ask the Holy Spirit daily, "How can I be a better servant for the Kingdom?" Jesus Christ gave his life, and I count it an honor to take communion. His death was reciprocity. There was an exchange of life and privileges granted to us while we're here on earth.

Paul wrote that communion should be taken for a specific purpose. He understood an exchange was to take place. My husband and I take communion as intercessors. We stand in the gap for our family. There were years of brokenness, abandonment, sickness and poverty that tried to attach itself to our family, but the devil is a LIAR! Those generational curses and strongholds have been broken. We take communion as reciprocity. Our family will walk in all that God has purposed for them in this life and in the next.

SACRED SPACE DOOR HANGER

And when thou prayest, thou shalt not be as the hypocrites are: for they love to pray standing in the synagogues and in the corners of the streets, that they may be seen of men. Verily I say unto you, They have their reward. But thou, when thou prayest, enter into thy closet, and when thou hast shut thy door, pray to thy Father which is in secret; and thy Father which seeth in secret shall reward thee openly (Matthew 6:5-6).

Personal prayer is meant to be private. There's a time and a place for corporate prayer, but there's also a time and place for personal prayer. Jesus is our example for building a powerful prayer life. The scripture often finds him alone, in the early morning dawn in prayer. This tells me a lot about how to model my prayer life.

First, He was always alone. He spent a lot of time with the disciples, yet he went to the garden alone. You need to have a sacred space for prayer. It may be an extra room in the house, a chair in the corner or a closet as long as you can have privacy. Your spouse and children must respect your personal prayer time with God. What God has for you is not meant for anyone else. Your spouse and children will have their personal relationship with the Holy Spirit.

When I pray, my husband never disturbs me. He knows I'm with the Holy Spirit. If I don't open the door, he waits. I'm glad we have that understanding that when my door is closed, it's sacred.

Many believers are not worshipers, and there's a difference. Exodus 8:1 the King James translation, says,

And the LORD spake unto Moses, Go unto Pharaoh, and say unto him, Thus saith the LORD, Let my people go, that they may serve [worhip] me.

Our active participation is expected. It is required. Worshiping requires a lifestyle change. I can't do the things I use to do, go to the places I use to go, say the things I use to say or think the way I use to think. There's a sacrifice you make as a worshiper that you don't make as a believer. Why? My active participation and exposure to the Word of God changes me.

In the Old Testament, the priest had access to the inner court and the Holy of Holies. That access required a lifestyle from them that God did not require of the others. God didn't just let anyone inside His sacred space.

It's still that way today. Even though the curtain was torn when Jesus died on the cross, access still requires sacrifice that has not changed. If you want to dwell inside the Holy of Holies, you have to move from just believing to worshiping. I've used everything in this box to help me make that transition. I no longer wanted to be on the outside wondering what it was like to have a relationship with God. I wanted to know for myself, so I made the commitment to do the work and start building that relationship. When I'm in my private place, I'm worshiping God!

Make sure your family understands what it means when you close the door. If they don't quite understand, that's okay as long as they don't disturb you.

BE CONSISTENT

Be consistent! I can't say that enough. Set aside the same time every day to meet up with the Holy Spirit. I have a standing appointment on my calendar at 4:30 am for prayer. I love to sleep in like the next person but remember we're modeling the things that we've read about Jesus Christ. He was an early morning prayer. I've chosen 4:30 because I always wanted to tithe the first fruit of my lips. I don't want to speak to anyone before I've had my personal prayer time with the Holy Spirit. My husband has to be up for work at 5:00 am. That means for me to get an hour of prayer before we connect in the morning, I need to be up at 4:30. By the time he showers and gets dressed it's 5:30 and I'm coming out of my office and making my way towards the kitchen. This is what sets the foundation of my day. This is how Jesus started his day.

The Word (which is Jesus Christ) thought it was important enough to get up, in the early morning dawn (before sunrise) to pray. He had private time (inside the Holy of Holies) with the Father (Creation itself) before he did anything. Matthew 6:33 says,

But seek ye first the kingdom of God, and his righteousness; and all these things shall be added unto you.

If you had an appointment on your calendar for a meeting with your boss at work, would you be late? Wouldn't you be prepared? Would you not show up? Well, if you don't keep your appointment with the Holy Spirit, that's exactly what you're doing, standing God up. Let me know how that works out for you.

Establishing a relationship involves sacrifice and work. I like to use my relationship with my husband as an example. I'm not telling you that this is a perfect relationship. What I'm giving you is an example of the amount of time it took to build a 37 years marriage.

In the morning, we have one-on-one face time. We spend a few minutes in the morning talking before we have prayer and communion. We love to send each other Marco Polo videos during the day. While he's at work we call one another, send text messages and use Facetime. There are even occasional emails during the day when we need to take care of business. Then when he comes home from work, there's more one-on-one face time together. That's building a relationship, constant communication.

God wants that same type of personal time with you. I'm always talking to him when I'm home alone. I'm up at 4:30am so I can have personal time with the Holy Spirit before I ever have any interaction with my husband. I set aside time for daily study before I pick up my phone or check emails. I pray before meals and discuss major decisions with the Holy Spirit. I've set aside 30 minutes in the evening to have more private time. Every night after my husband falls asleep; I put my ear buds in and doze off listening to my audio Bible. My benchmark has always been two hours and forty minutes. That's the goal, to tithe a tenth of my day.

Remember, any long-lasting relationship requires sacrifice. It will require commitment, trust and an enormous investment of your time.

KLEENEX TISSUE

Now the Kleenex tissues are pretty simple. They're for the many tears you'll shed while in the presence of the Holy Spirit. This is just a starter kit, trust me you'll need a much bigger box.

KEEPSAKE BOX

This keepsake box was handmade and designed especially for THE PRAYER BOX. The box is great for storing mementos from a wedding, birthday or graduation. But most importantly, it can be used to store your prayer journals. In time, you'll be able to go back and read all of the promises God has kept in His covenant with you.

CHAPTER 3

SCRIPTURES FOR WEEKLY ASSIGNMENTS

When you pray and begin to seek the Face of God, your life will change. Change can only happen when you're honest with yourself, when you're willing to address the deep-rooted brokenness in your heart. Change can happen when you're open to releasing years of resentment and unforgiveness towards those who've hurt you. Yes, change can happen but only when you stop allowing the precious real estate of your mind to be occupied by unauthorized squatters. Romans 12:2 says,

And be not conformed to this world: but be ye transformed by the renewing of your mind, that ye may prove what [is] that good, and acceptable, and perfect, will of God.

You cannot get on your knees, quote a bunch of scriptures, get up and keep doing the same things you use to do and expect different results. Your active participation in changing your heart posture is expected. It's required.

Most people pray in hopes of changing the people or circumstance around them. If you pray in hopes of changing yourself, the people around you and even the circumstances will change. Why? You'll begin to see them in a different way. Now, I didn't say it would be all good news. Sometimes the change you'll see is your spiritual eyes exposing you to the truth. The truth can hurt, but it will also set you free.

I have someone who is near and dear to me, who believes that every sermon they hear and every prayer that's prayed is about fixing the other person. They struggle to take ownership and accept that prayer is for them. If you cannot be honest with yourself, while you're on your knees in the Presence of God, then the road ahead of you will be difficult.

I've learned over the years that unless I'm led by the Holy Spirit to pray for someone else, that the prayers he puts on my heart to pray are meant for me. I welcome the growth and maturity in my life.

Over the next four weeks, part of your assignment will be to pick one, no more than two scriptures to meditate on for the entire week. Some people like to choose daily scriptures, and that's fine, but I've found there is more revelation and power when I sit with one or two verses each week.

Pray over the scriptures and ask the Holy Spirit to give you revelation and clarity about how to apply the scripture to your life. If you're just reading your Bible without prayer, you're essentially reading a novel. That's like a soldier that carries around a gun and never loads it with bullets. What's the point?

The Bible is full of revelation but the only way to receive it is through prayer. Start doing it every day before you read, and you'll see what I mean. As you begin to pray over your Bible, it begins to reveal its secrets to you. Your understanding of the scriptures will completely change; it's the most powerful experience ever!

Below are some of my favorite Bible scriptures. I've selected these scriptures because they're important to building and shoring up your foundation. Some of these may be new to you and some of these you may already know. These scriptures cover the battlefield of the mind, communion, influence, prayer, praise, reverence and worship. To be honest, all of these scriptures in this book should be staples in your prayer life. Trust me; you'll need them all!

LESSONS

1. Pick one, no more than two scriptures each week.

2. Pray over the scriptures and then read and meditate on them daily.

3. Ask the Holy Spirit to bring you clarity and direction on how to apply the scriptures you've chosen to your life.

4. Make sure to write down any revelation that the Holy Spirit gives you (use your red ink pen).

5. Develop the habit of looking up the definition of every word in the scripture, even if you think you know what it means. There's power in knowledge and what you'll find will amaze you.

SCRIPTURES

Battlefield of the Mind

Romans 12:2 - *And be not conformed to this world: but be ye transformed by the renewing of your mind, that ye may prove what [is] that good, and acceptable, and perfect, will of God.*

~

2 Corinthians 10:3-5 - *For though we walk in the flesh, we do not war after the flesh: (For the weapons of our warfare are not carnal, but mighty through God to the pulling down of strong holds;) Casting down imaginations, and every high thing that exalteth itself against the knowledge of God, and bringing into captivity every thought to the obedience of Christ;*

~

2 Corinthians 10:5 - *Casting down imaginations, and every high thing that exalteth itself against the knowledge of God, and bringing into captivity every thought to the obedience of Christ;*

~

Isaiah 26:3 - *Thou wilt keep [him] in perfect peace, [whose] mind [is] stayed [on thee]: because he trusteth in thee.*

~

Philippians 4:6-8 – *Be careful for nothing; but in every thing by prayer and supplication with thanksgiving let your requests be made known unto God. And the peace of God, which passeth all understanding, shall keep your hearts and minds through Christ Jesus. Finally, brethren, whatsoever things are true, whatsoever things are honest, whatsoever things are just, whatsoever things are pure, whatsoever things are lovely, whatsoever things are of good report; if there be any virtue, and if there be any praise, think on these things.*

Ephesians 6:12 - For we wrestle not against flesh and blood, but against principalities, against powers, against the rulers of the darkness of this world, against spiritual wickedness in high [places].

~

James 4:7 - Submit yourselves therefore to God. Resist the devil, and he will flee from you.

~

2 Corinthians 10:4 - (For the weapons of our warfare [are] not carnal, but mighty through God to the pulling down of strong holds).

~

Psalms 27:1 - ([A Psalm] of David.) The LORD [is] my light and my salvation; whom shall I fear? the LORD [is] the strength of my life; of whom shall I be afraid?

~

Hebrews 13:5 - [Let your] conversation [be] without covetousness; [and be] content with such things as ye have: for he hath said, I will never leave thee, nor forsake thee.

~

Colossians 1:13 - Who hath delivered us from the power of darkness, and hath translated [us] into the kingdom of his dear Son:

~

John 8:32 - And ye shall know the truth, and the truth shall make you free.

~

Psalms 91:1 - He that dwelleth in the secret place of the Most High shall abide under the shadow of the Almighty.

Romans 8:13 - *For if ye live after the flesh, ye shall die: but if ye through the Spirit do mortify the deeds of the body, ye shall live.*

~

2 Timothy 1:7 - *For God hath not given us the spirit of fear; but of power, and of love, and of a sound mind.*

~

Proverbs 16:18 - *Pride [goeth] before destruction, and a haughty spirit before a fall.*

~

1 John 3:9 - *Whosoever is born of God doth not commit sin; for his seed remaineth in him: and he cannot sin, because he is born of God.*

~

Mark 4:24 - *And he said unto them, Take heed what ye hear: with what measure ye mete, it shall be measured to you: and unto you that hear shall more be given.*

~

Romans 8:37 - *Nay, in all these things we are more than conquerors through him that loved us.*

~

Romans 8:1 - *[There is] therefore now no condemnation to them which are in Christ Jesus, who walk not after the flesh, but after the Spirit.*

~

Luke 4:18 - *The Spirit of the Lord [is] upon me, because he hath anointed me to preach the gospel to the poor; he hath sent me to heal the brokenhearted, to preach deliverance to the captives, and recovering of sight to the blind, to set at liberty them that are bruised.*

Communion

1 Corinthians 11:26 - *For as often as ye eat this bread, and drink this cup, ye do shew the Lord's death till he comes.*

~

Matthew 26:26-28 - *And as they were eating, Jesus took bread, and blessed it, and brake it, and gave it to the disciples, and said, Take, eat; this is my body. And he took the cup, and gave thanks, and gave it to them, saying, Drink ye all of it; For this is my blood of the new testament, which is shed for many for the remission of sins.*

~

Acts 20:7 - *And upon the first [day] of the week, when the disciples came together to break bread, Paul preached unto them, ready to depart on the morrow; and continued his speech until midnight.*

~

1 Corinthians 11:25 - *After the same manner also [he took] the cup, when he had supped, saying, This cup is the new testament in my blood: this do ye, as oft as ye drink [it], in remembrance of me.*

~

1 Corinthians 10:17 - *For we [being] many are one bread, [and] one body: for we are all partakers of that one bread.*

~

Acts 2:42 - *And they continued steadfastly in the apostles' doctrine and fellowship, and in the breaking of bread, and in prayers.*

~

1 Corinthians 11:24 - *And when he had given thanks, he brake [it], and said, Take, eat: this is my body, which is broken for you: this do in remembrance of me.*

John 6:53-58 – *Then Jesus said unto them, Verily, verily, I say unto you, Except ye eat the flesh of the Son of man, and drink his blood, ye have no life in you. Whoso eateth my flesh, and drinketh my blood, hath eternal life; and I will raise him up at the last day. For my flesh is meat indeed, and my blood is drink indeed. He that eateth my flesh, and drinketh my blood, dwelleth in me, and I in him. As the living Father hath sent me, and I live by the Father: so he that eateth me, even he shall live by me. This is that bread which came down from heaven: not as your fathers did eat manna, and are dead: he that eateth of this bread shall live forever.*

~

1 Corinthians 10:16 - *The cup of blessing which we bless, is it not the communion of the blood of Christ? The bread which we break, is it not the communion of the body of Christ?*

~

Luke 22:19-20 - *And he took bread, and gave thanks, and brake it, and gave unto them, saying, This is my body, which is given for you: this do in remembrance of me. Likewise also the cup after supper, saying, This cup is the new testament in my blood, which is shed for you.*

~

1 John 1:3 - *That which we have seen and heard declare we unto you, that ye also may have fellowship with us: and truly our fellowship [is] with the Father, and with his Son Jesus Christ.*

~

Mark 14:22-25 – *And as they did eat, Jesus took bread, and blessed, and brake it, and gave to them, and said, Take, eat: this is my body. And he took the cup, and when he had given thanks, he gave it to them: and they all drank of it. And he said unto them, This is my blood of the new testament, which is shed for many. Verily I say unto you, I will drink no more of the fruit of the vine, until that day that I drink it new in the kingdom of God.*

Influence

Matthew 5:13-16 – *Ye are the salt of the earth: but if the salt has lost his savour, wherewith shall it be salted? it is thenceforth good for nothing, but to be cast* out, and to be trodden under foot of men. Ye are the light of the world. A city that is set on a hill cannot be hidden. Neither do men light a candle, and put it under a bushel, but on a candlestick; and it giveth light unto all that are in the house. Let your light so shine before men, that they may see your good works, and glorify your Father which is in heaven.

~

1 Corinthians 15:33 - Be not deceived: evil communications corrupt good manners.

~

Proverbs 27:17 - Iron sharpeneth iron; so a man sharpeneth the countenance of his friend.

~

Proverbs 13:20 - He that walketh with wise [men] shall be wise: but a companion of fools shall be destroyed.

~

1 Peter 3:16 - Having a good conscience; that, whereas they speak evil of you, as of evildoers, they may be ashamed that falsely accuse your good conversation in Christ.

~

1 Peter 2:12 - Having your conversation honest among the Gentiles: that, whereas they speak against you as evildoers, they may by [your] good works, which they shall behold, glorify God in the day of visitation.

~

Proverbs 9:9 - Give [instruction] to a wise [man], and he will be yet wiser: teach a just [man], and he will increase in learning.

Proverbs 10:17 - He [is in] the way of life that keepeth instruction: but he that refuseth reproof erreth.

~

1 Peter 3:15 - But sanctify the Lord God in your hearts: and [be] ready always to [give] an answer to every man that asketh you a reason of the hope that is in you with meekness and fear:

~

2 Timothy 3:16-17 - All scripture [is] given by inspiration of God, and [is] profitable for doctrine, for reproof, for correction, for instruction in righteousness: That the man of God may be perfect, thoroughly furnished unto all good works.

~

Proverbs 19:6 - Many will intreat the favour of the prince: and every man [is] a friend to him that giveth gifts.

~

Proverbs 22:24 - Make no friendship with an angry man; and with a furious man thou shalt not go:

~

Proverbs 15:1 - A soft answer turneth away wrath: but grievous words stir up anger.

Morning Prayer

Psalms 90:14 - O satisfy us early with thy mercy; that we may rejoice and be glad all our days.

~

Psalms 5:3 - My voice shalt thou hear in the morning, O LORD; in the morning will I direct [my prayer] unto thee, and will look up.

Mark 1:35 - *And in the morning, rising up a great while before day, he went out, and departed into a solitary place, and there prayed.*

~

Psalms 63:1-11 - *O God, thou [art] my God; early will I seek thee: my soul thirsteth for thee.*

~

Psalms 57:8 - *Awake up, my glory; awake, psaltery and harp: I [myself] will awake early.*

~

Job 38:12 - *Hast thou commanded the morning since thy days; [and] caused the dayspring to know his place;*

~

Proverbs 8:17 - *I love them that love me; and those that seek me early shall find me.*

~

Exodus 34:2 - *And be ready in the morning, and come up in the morning unto mount Sinai, and present thyself there to me in the top of the mount.*

~

Joshua 6:15 - *And it came to pass on the seventh day, that they rose early about the dawning of the day, and compassed the city after the same manner seven times: only on that day they compassed the city seven times.*

Prayer

Psalms 34:17 - *[The righteous] cry, and the LORD heareth, and delivereth them out of all their troubles.*

Jeremiah 33:3 - *Call unto me, and I will answer thee, and shew thee great and mighty things, which thou knowest not.*

~

Matthew 6:5 - *And when thou prayest, thou shalt not be as the hypocrites [are]: for they love to pray standing in the synagogues and in the corners of the streets, that they may be seen of men. Verily I say unto you, They have their reward.*

~

Matthew 6:6 - *But thou, when thou prayest, enter into thy closet, and when thou hast shut thy door, pray to thy Father which is in secret; and thy Father which seeth in secret shall reward thee openly.*

Matthew 6:7 - *But when ye pray, use not vain repetitions, as the heathen [do]: for they think that they shall be heard for their much speaking.*

~

Matthew 6:9-13 - *After this manner therefore pray ye: Our Father which art in heaven, Hallowed be thy name. Thy kingdom come, Thy will be done in earth, as it is in heaven. Give us this day our daily bread. And forgive us our debts, as we forgive our debtors. And lead us not into temptation, but deliver us from evil: For thine is the kingdom, and the power, and the glory, for ever. Amen.*

~

Matthew 26:41 - *Watch and pray, that ye enter not into temptation: the spirit indeed [is] willing, but the flesh [is] weak.*

~

Mark 11:24 - *Therefore I say unto you, What things so ever ye desire, when ye pray, believe that ye receive [them], and ye shall have [them].*

~

Luke 11:9 - *And I say unto you, Ask, and it shall be given you; seek, and ye shall find; knock, and it shall be opened unto you.*

Luke 18:1 - And he spake a parable unto them [to this end], that men ought always to pray, and not to faint;

~

John 15:7 - If ye abide in me, and my words abide in you, ye shall ask what ye will, and it shall be done unto you.

~

Romans 8:26 - Likewise the Spirit also helpeth our infirmities: for we know not what we should pray for as we ought: but the Spirit itself maketh intercession for us with groanings which cannot be uttered.

~

Ephesians 6:18 - Praying always with all prayer and supplication in the Spirit, and watching thereunto with all perseverance and supplication for all saints;

~

Philippians 4:6 - Be careful for nothing; but in every thing by prayer and supplication with thanksgiving let your requests be made known unto God.

~

1 Thessalonians 5:17 - Pray without ceasing.

~

1 Timothy 2:5 - For [there is] one God, and one mediator between God and men, the man Christ Jesus;

~

James 5:16 - Confess [your] faults one to another, and pray one for another, that ye may be healed. The effectual fervent prayer of a righteous man availeth much.

Praise

Psalms 150:1 - *Praise ye the LORD. Praise God in his sanctuary: praise him in the firmament of his power.*

~

John 4:23 - *But the hour cometh, and now is, when the true worshippers shall worship the Father in spirit and in truth: for the Father seeketh such to worship him.*

~

Psalms 100:2 - *Serve the LORD with gladness: come before his presence with singing.*

Psalms 150:6 - *Let every thing that hath breath praise the LORD. Praise ye the LORD.*

~

Psalms 95:1-6 - *O come, let us sing unto the LORD: let us make a joyful noise to the rock of our salvation. Let us come before his presence with thanksgiving, and make a joyful noise unto him with psalms. For the Lord is a great God, and a great King above all gods. In his hand are the deep places of the earth: the strength of the hills is his also. The sea is his, and he made it: and his hands formed the dry land. O come, let us worship and bow down: let us kneel before the Lord our maker.*

~

Colossians 3:16 - *Let the word of Christ dwell in you richly in all wisdom; teaching and admonishing one another in psalms and hymns and spiritual songs, singing with grace in your hearts to the Lord.*

~

Hebrews 13:15 - *By him therefore let us offer the sacrifice of praise to God continually, that is, the fruit of [our] lips giving thanks to his name.*

Psalms 117:1-2 - O praise the LORD, all ye nations; praise him, all ye people. For his merciful kindness is great toward us: and the truth of the Lord endureth for ever. Praise ye the Lord.

~

Psalms 100:4 - Enter into his gates with thanksgiving, [and] into his courts with praise: be thankful unto him, [and] bless his name.

~

Psalms 96:1 - O sing unto the LORD a new song: sing unto the LORD, all the earth.

Zephaniah 3:17 - The LORD thy God in the midst of thee [is] mighty; he will save, he will rejoice over thee with joy; he will rest in his love, he will joy over thee with singing.

~

John 4:24 - God [is] a Spirit: and they that worship him must worship [him] in spirit and in truth.

~

Ephesians 5:19 - Speaking to yourselves in psalms and hymns and spiritual songs, singing and making melody in your heart to the Lord;

~

Psalms 146:1 - Praise ye the LORD. Praise the LORD, O my soul.

~

Psalms 30:11 - Thou hast turned for me my mourning into dancing: thou hast put off my sackcloth, and girded me with gladness.

Psalms 149:3 - *Let them praise his name in the dance: let them sing praises unto him with the timbrel and harp.*

<u>Reverence</u>

Hebrews 12:28 - *Wherefore we receiving a kingdom which cannot be moved, let us have grace, whereby we may serve God acceptably with reverence and godly fear:*

~

Exodus 3:5 - *And he said, Draw not nigh hither: put off thy shoes from off thy feet, for the place whereon thou standest [is] holy ground.*

1 Samuel 12:24 - *Only fear the LORD, and serve him in truth with all your heart: for consider how great [things] he hath done for you.*

~

Hebrews 5:7 - *Who in the days of his flesh, when he had offered up prayers and supplications with strong crying and tears unto him that was able to save him from death, and was heard in that he feared;*

<u>Worship</u>

Psalms 29:2 - *Give unto the LORD the glory due unto his name; worship the LORD in the beauty of holiness.*

~

Psalms 95:6 - *O come, let us worship and bow down: let us kneel before the LORD our maker.*

~

Isaiah 12:5 - *Sing unto the LORD; for he hath done excellent things: this [is] known in all the earth.*

Luke 4:8 - *And Jesus answered and said unto him, Get thee behind me, Satan: for it is written, Thou shalt worship the Lord thy God, and him only shalt thou serve.*

~

John 4:23 - *But the hour cometh, and now is, when the true worshippers shall worship the Father in spirit and in truth: for the Father seeketh such to worship him.*

~

John 4:24 - *God [is] a Spirit: and they that worship him must worship [him] in spirit and in truth.*

Romans 12:1 - *I beseech you therefore, brethren, by the mercies of God, that ye present your bodies a living sacrifice, holy, acceptable unto God, [which is] your reasonable service.*

~

Colossians 3:14 - *And above all these things [put on] charity, which is the bond of perfectness.*

~

Hebrews 13:15 - *By him therefore let us offer the sacrifice of praise to God continually, that is, the fruit of [our] lips giving thanks to his name.*

CHAPTER 4

MORNING PRAISE PLAYLIST

Praise and worship music has a way of penetrating your heart, spirit, soul, and body. It can reach down to the brokenness in the marrow of your bones. Joel Houston, Hillsong United member, says, "Music has the ability to enter someone's soul without their permission."

I couldn't agree more. The effects of music reach much farther than our eardrums. Music can change your mood, open your mind and can even turn your unforgiving heart around.

Growing up, my father loved music. He'd listened to just about anything with a beat. He loved R&B, Jazz, Country and Western, and even a little Rock and Roll but he drew the line on Classical music. On Sundays, we'd listened to Gospel music. His collection included Mahalia Jackson, Aretha Franklin, James Cleveland, Edwin Hawkins, and Elvis Presley. All on vinyl records of course. I'd sit for hours staring at the album jackets. I'm so thankful for those memories. This was my introduction to Gospel music

I've created a playlist for you on SPOTIFY under the username, MARY ESTHER RUTH. The playlist has some of my favorite praise and worship songs. I've included artist like All Sons and Daughters, Anthony Brown & Group Therapy, Chris Tomlin, Casey J, Elevation Worship, Israel Houghton, Mercy Me, Phil Wickham, Psalmist Raine, Tasha Cobbs Leonard, Travis Green, Jesus Culture, Hillsong, and many more amazing artists. Currently there are 100 songs on our playlist for you to choose from and we will continue to add to the list.

- **Go to:** SPOTIFY (spotify.com)
- **Username:** MARY ESTHER RUTH
- **Playlist:** THE PRAYER BOX MORNING PRAISE

LESSON

1. Pick one, no more than two praise and worship songs for the week. I usually just sit with one song. I've been able to discern over the years that when I'm really struggling or entering deep warfare I tend to draw on praise and worship songs quite a bit.

2. Let the song and the words minister to you.

3. Make sure to write down any revelation that the Holy Spirit gives you (use your red ink pen).

CHAPTER 5

BE DOERS

We don't want to be just hearers of the Word; we want our lives to testify that we are doers of the Word of God. James 1:22 says, *"But be ye doers of the word, and not hearers only, deceiving your own selves."*

So now you have all you need to get started. Let's recap.

- We know we're soldiers for the Kingdom, and we're about to start our basic training.
- We know the definition of prayer:
  - Prayer is talking to God
- We know the purpose of prayer:
  - Prayer is supernatural communication
  - Prayer is influence
  - Prayer is a weapon
  - Pray boldly
- We have our prayer box essentials:
  - Prayer pillow and our different prayer postures
  - Journal and black and red pens
  - Prayer Guide
  - Weekly Communion
  - Sacred Space Door Hanger
  - You have a standing appointment on your calendar.
  - You have your sacred space identified
  - Kleenex Tissue
  - Keepsake Box to store all of our prayer journals

- We have scriptures that prepare us for spiritual warfare:
  - Battlefield in our mind
  - Communion
  - Influence
  - Prayer
  - Praise
    - Reverence
    - Worship

- We have our praise and worship playlist
- We have our Bible.

A couple of things you don't need to worry about:
- Don't spend time worrying about using the right words or theological terminologies. Enter His gates with Thanksgiving and His courts with praise. Ask the Holy Spirit what would He like for you to pray. Prayer is about surrendering your spirit so you can pray as the Holy Spirit directs you. This will amaze you!
- Don't spend time doubting that this will work. There is NO quick, fast way to build a relationship with God. It's you putting into practice good prayer habits. It's just like building good work habits. The rest will come.

Now that you're ready to start the work, let's say a prayer together.

Dear Heavenly Father,

We kneel before you today giving you all the glory and praise due to the King of kings. We call it an honour to worship you and to sing your praises.

Father, we are willing to commit in our heart, mind, and spirit to do the work needed to enrich our relationship with you. Being a Believer is not enough. We come to you today as Worshippers. We surrender our will to your Will.

We release anything that is not of you, by you, from you or through you in our lives. We take up our cross and fight as soldiers for the Kingdom. We repent of all our wrong doings and release anyone that we've held in offense. We want nothing hidden in the deepest parts of our hearts that could separate us from you.

As we study Your Word, Father, we ask that you give us the wisdom that we lack in our understanding. Your Word says that if we lack wisdom and we ask you for it, you'll give it to us liberally and not hold it against us. We ask for that wisdom today in the name of Christ Jesus that we may be wise soldiers for your kingdom!

We ask that your Word penetrate every fiber of our being down to the marrow of our bone. We ask that you bury your Word deep in our hearts so that as we fight as soldiers we'll always have the ability to recall the Word of God.

We ask these things in the name of Christ Jesus our Lord and Saviour. Amen!

LET'S GET STARTED!

CHAPTER 6

WEEK ONE ASSIGNMENT

Foundations are the lowest load-bearing part of any structure. The foundation of a building transfers all of the weight of that structure to the ground or earth below. They're usually made out of stone or concrete and can support significant weight. The taller the vertical structure on top the deeper the foundation on the bottom. It is the same with God.

Pouring a foundation for a building or a house takes time and it's not something that a builder will rush to do. Any good construction manager knows the success of the project is tied to the foundation. Foundation repairs can be difficult to fix and are very expensive. It does not matter how amazing the building looks if it has foundation issues.

Over the next 30 days you'll focus on the most important part of any relationship, the foundation. You're learning the importance of the load-bearing structure that carries your faith. The deeper you go in with God the taller your faith. As you begin to work through your daily assignments you'll notice that every day you have the same routine. That's basic training.

The first couple of weeks are always the hardest because you're attacking old habits to make room for new ones. You're excavating things that can destroy your foundation (old wounds, relationships, untruths, outright lies, and much more). You're digging, removing and filling in holes all at the same time. If your foundation is not right the whole building can crumble.

Basic training is not easy. You're preparing yourself mentally, physically and emotionally. It's sole purpose it to make you stronger. It is the foundation for the soldier. Building strong spiritual disciplines will make you stronger. You're building good habits that will support you for the rest of your earthly life.

Usually, after excavating the land you are ready for the footings. The footings are the load carriers. They are strategically placed to support the weight and size of the house or building. Footings also take into consideration the soil conditions that surround the house.

That's what you're experiencing right now in basic training. You're excavating and pouring your footings. You're doing it by showing up on time. Strategically finding a time and place to meet with the Holy Spirit. You're checking your heart posture and removing old weeds, broken branches or old concrete from an old broken foundation. You're spending time studying scriptures that will help you shore up the new foundation you're laying. Scriptures are your footings. They'll help you carry the weight. Study your scriptures don't just memorize them. You'll need them and when you do you want to call on them from the depths of your soul.

During any basic training program your drill sergeant will have great cadences for you to march to. I wanted to leave you with one as well. If you're not familiar with the marching process, military cadences were used years ago as troops marched into battle. Today, they're used primarily for marching exercises. Cadences help keep the troops in step so they can land their feet at the same time.

I want you to have a cadence to march to so that you will know you are not alone in this process. We may not be together physically, but we are spiritually. You are now a part of The Prayer Box community. We are all landing our feet at the exact same time and we're causing a prideful beat for the Kingdom.

Don't forget to listen to the daily podcast. I'm right here with you!

Week One Cadence: "Fired Up"

Fired up
Fired up

Motivated
Motivated

Dedicated
Dedicated

On my knees
On my knees

Daily
Daily

Praying to God
Praying to God

Forgive me
Forgive me

I'm doing it right
I'm doing it right

I'm kneeling low
I'm kneeling low

I'm going high
I'm going high

Here I go
Here I go

Fired up, Fired up, Fired up!

"Fired Up" is a military cadence. No information on author or origin. This cadence has been rewritten by Paula Bryant-Ellis.

WEEK ONE - DAY ONE

Start Time: _____ **AM/PM**

Did you add your appointment with the Holy Spirit to your daily calendar? Make it a recurring appointment with no ending date.

How long did you pray: _____ **MINUTES/HOURS**

Start with a minimum of 15-20 minutes and work your way up from there by adding 5-10 minutes each week. I want you to get in the habit of spending time with the Holy Spirit. Show up on time and be consistent. Just like with any relationship, the more time you spend together, the more intimacy and trust you have in the relationship.

Did you take your communion for the week? YES / NO

What's your reason for taking communion this week? What are you asking the Holy Spirit to do or to change in your life?

_____

_____

_____

What scripture(s) did you select for the week? What spiritual warfare are you in right now; battling the mind and being focused, taking communion (make sure your heart posture is pure), needing influence and favor, consistent prayer life, humility in your praise, complete surrender in reverence and worship?

Scripture #1

_____

_____

_____

_____

Scripture #2

_____

_____

_____

Always start your prayer time with praise and worship (you don't always have to use music for praise and worship). **What song did you select today, if any?**

_____

_____

Was there anything in particular that you needed from the song you selected? When I'm in a dry place or in a deep battle, I need music to help me start my mornings. But you will get to a place that you won't need music to help you enter into His Presence. Once you start spending quality time together, you just enter in and start praising Him and the tears will begin to flow.

_____

_____

_____

What did you pray about today (make sure to write it in **BLACK** ink)? **What direction or revelation did the Holy Spirit give you today?** Start dedicating at least 10 minutes after prayer to just sit in complete quietness and listen to the Voice of the Holy Spirit (make sure to write it in **RED** ink). **Were you able to release anything that was hindering you from spending time in the Presence of God?**

_____

_____

_____

WEEK ONE - DAY TWO

Start Time: _____ **AM/PM**

Did you add your appointment with the Holy Spirit to your daily calendar? Make it a recurring appointment with no ending date.

How long did you pray: _____ **MINUTES/HOURS**

Start with a minimum of 15-20 minutes, and work your way up from there by adding 5-10 minutes each week. I want you to get in the habit of spending time with the Holy Spirit. Show up on time and be consistent. Just like with any relationship, the more time you spend together, the more intimacy and trust you have in the relationship.

What scripture(s) did you select for the week?

What spiritual warfare are you in right now; battling the mind and being focused, taking communion (make sure your heart posture is pure), needing influence and favor, consistent prayer life, humility in your praise, complete surrender in reverence and worship?

Scripture #1

_____

_____

_____

Scripture #2

_____

_____

_____

_____

Always start your prayer time with praise and worship (you don't always have to use music for praise and worship). **What song did you select today, if any?**

_____

_____

Was there anything in particular that you needed from the song you selected? When I'm in a dry place or in a deep battle, I need music to help me start my mornings. But you will get to a place that you won't need music to help you enter into His Presence. Once you start spending quality time together, you just enter in and start praising Him and the tears will begin to flow.

_____

_____

_____

_____

What did you pray about today (make sure to write it in **BLACK** ink)**? What direction or revelation did the Holy Spirit give you today?** Start dedicating at least 10 minutes after prayer to just sit in complete quietness and listen to the Voice of the Holy Spirit (make sure to write it in **RED** ink). **Were you able to release anything that was hindering you from spending time in the Presence of God?**

_____

_____

_____

_____

_____

_____

WEEK ONE - DAY THREE

Start Time: _____ **AM/PM**

Did you add your appointment with the Holy Spirit to your daily calendar? Make it a recurring appointment with no ending date.

How long did you pray: _____ **MINUTES/HOURS**

Start with a minimum of 15-20 minutes, and work your way up from there by adding 5-10 minutes each week. I want you to get in the habit of spending time with the Holy Spirit. Show up on time and be consistent. Just like with any relationship, the more time you spend together, the more intimacy and trust you have in the relationship.

What scripture(s) did you select for the week?

What spiritual warfare are you in right now; battling the mind and being focused, taking communion (make sure your heart posture is pure), needing influence and favor, consistent prayer life, humility in your praise, complete surrender in reverence and worship?

Scripture #1

_____

_____

_____

Scripture #2

_____

_____

_____

_____

Always start your prayer time with praise and worship (you don't always have to use music for praise and worship). **What song did you select today, if any?**

_____

_____

Was there anything in particular that you needed from the song you selected? When I'm in a dry place or in a deep battle, I need music to help me start my mornings. But you will get to a place that you won't need music to help you enter into His Presence. Once you start spending quality time together, you just enter in and start praising Him and the tears will begin to flow.

_____

_____

_____

_____

What did you pray about today (make sure to write it in **BLACK** ink)**? What direction or revelation did the Holy Spirit give you today?** Start dedicating at least 10 minutes after prayer to just sit in complete quietness and listen to the Voice of the Holy Spirit (make sure to write it in **RED** ink). **Were you able to release anything that was hindering you from spending time in the Presence of God?**

_____

_____

_____

_____

_____

WEEK ONE - DAY FOUR

Start Time: _____ **AM/PM**

Did you add your appointment with the Holy Spirit to your daily calendar? Make it a recurring appointment with no ending date.

How long did you pray: _____ **MINUTES/HOURS**

Start with a minimum of 15-20 minutes, and work your way up from there by adding 5-10 minutes each week. I want you to get in the habit of spending time with the Holy Spirit. Show up on time and be consistent. Just like with any relationship, the more time you spend together, the more intimacy and trust you have in the relationship.

What scripture(s) did you select for the week?

What spiritual warfare are you in right now; battling the mind and being focused, taking communion (make sure your heart posture is pure), needing influence and favor, consistent prayer life, humility in your praise, complete surrender in reverence and worship?

Scripture #1

_____

_____

_____

Scripture #2

_____

_____

_____

_____

Always start your prayer time with praise and worship (you don't always have to use music for praise and worship). **What song did you select today, if any?**

_____

_____

_____

Was there anything in particular that you needed from the song you selected? When I'm in a dry place or in a deep battle, I need music to help me start my mornings. But you will get to a place that you won't need music to help you enter into His Presence. Once you start spending quality time together, you just enter in and start praising Him and the tears will begin to flow.

_____

_____

_____

What did you pray about today (make sure to write it in **BLACK** ink)**? What direction or revelation did the Holy Spirit give you today?** Start dedicating at least 10 minutes after prayer to just sit in complete quietness and listen to the Voice of the Holy Spirit (make sure to write it in **RED** ink). **Were you able to release anything that was hindering you from spending time in the Presence of God?**

_____

_____

_____

_____

_____

_____

WEEK ONE · DAY FIVE

Start Time: _____ **AM/PM**

Did you add your appointment with the Holy Spirit to your daily calendar? Make it a recurring appointment with no ending date.

How long did you pray: _____ **MINUTES/HOURS**

Start with a minimum of 15-20 minutes, and work your way up from there by adding 5-10 minutes each week. I want you to get in the habit of spending time with the Holy Spirit. Show up on time and be consistent. Just like with any relationship, the more time you spend together, the more intimacy and trust you have in the relationship.

What scripture(s) did you select for the week?

What spiritual warfare are you in right now; battling the mind and being focused, taking communion (make sure your heart posture is pure), needing influence and favor, consistent prayer life, humility in your praise, complete surrender in reverence and worship?

Scripture #1

_____

_____

_____

Scripture #2

_____

_____

_____

_____

Always start your prayer time with praise and worship (you don't always have to use music for praise and worship). **What song did you select today, if any?**

_____

_____

Was there anything in particular that you needed from the song you selected? When I'm in a dry place or in a deep battle, I need music to help me start my mornings. But you will get to a place that you won't need music to help you enter into His Presence. Once you start spending quality time together, you just enter in and start praising Him and the tears will begin to flow.

_____

_____

_____

_____

What did you pray about today (make sure to write it in **BLACK** ink)? **What direction or revelation did the Holy Spirit give you today?** Start dedicating at least 10 minutes after prayer to just sit in complete quietness and listen to the Voice of the Holy Spirit (make sure to write it in **RED** ink). **Were you able to release anything that was hindering you from spending time in the Presence of God?**

_____

_____

_____

_____

_____

_____

WEEK ONE - DAY SIX

Start Time: _____ **AM/PM**

Did you add your appointment with the Holy Spirit to your daily calendar? Make it a recurring appointment with no ending date.

How long did you pray: _____ **MINUTES/HOURS**

Start with a minimum of 15-20 minutes, and work your way up from there by adding 5-10 minutes each week. I want you to get in the habit of spending time with the Holy Spirit. Show up on time and be consistent. Just like with any relationship, the more time you spend together, the more intimacy and trust you have in the relationship.

What scripture(s) did you select for the week?

What spiritual warfare are you in right now; battling the mind and being focused, taking communion (make sure your heart posture is pure), needing influence and favor, consistent prayer life, humility in your praise, complete surrender in reverence and worship?

Scripture #1

_____

_____

_____

Scripture #2

_____

_____

_____

_____

Always start your prayer time with praise and worship (you don't always have to use music for praise and worship). **What song did you select today, if any?**

_____

_____

Was there anything in particular that you needed from the song you selected? When I'm in a dry place or in a deep battle, I need music to help me start my mornings. But you will get to a place that you won't need music to help you enter into His Presence. Once you start spending quality time together, you just enter in and start praising Him and the tears will begin to flow.

_____

_____

_____

What did you pray about today (make sure to write it in **BLACK** ink)? **What direction or revelation did the Holy Spirit give you today?** Start dedicating at least 10 minutes after prayer to just sit in complete quietness and listen to the Voice of the Holy Spirit (make sure to write it in **RED** ink). **Were you able to release anything that was hindering you from spending time in the Presence of God?**

_____

_____

_____

_____

_____

WEEK ONE   DAY SEVEN

Start Time: _____ **AM/PM**

Did you add your appointment with the Holy Spirit to your daily calendar? Make it a recurring appointment with no ending date.

How long did you pray: _____ **MINUTES/HOURS**

Start with a minimum of 15-20 minutes, and work your way up from there by adding 5-10 minutes each week. I want you to get in the habit of spending time with the Holy Spirit. Show up on time and be consistent. Just like with any relationship, the more time you spend together, the more intimacy and trust you have in the relationship.

What scripture(s) did you select for the week?

What spiritual warfare are you in right now; battling the mind and being focused, taking communion (make sure your heart posture is pure), needing influence and favor, consistent prayer life, humility in your praise, complete surrender in reverence and worship?

Scripture #1

_____

_____

_____

Scripture #2

_____

_____

_____

Always start your prayer time with praise and worship (you don't always have to use music for praise and worship). **What song did you select today, if any?**

_____

_____

Was there anything in particular that you needed from the song you selected? When I'm in a dry place or in a deep battle, I need music to help me start my mornings. But you will get to a place that you won't need music to help you enter into His Presence. Once you start spending quality time together, you just enter in and start praising Him and the tears will begin to flow.

_____

_____

_____

_____

What did you pray about today (make sure to write it in **BLACK** ink)? **What direction or revelation did the Holy Spirit give you today?** Start dedicating at least 10 minutes after prayer to just sit in complete quietness and listen to the Voice of the Holy Spirit (make sure to write it in **RED** ink). **Were you able to release anything that was hindering you from spending time in the Presence of God?**

_____

_____

_____

_____

_____

_____

CHAPTER 7

WEEK TWO ASSIGNMENT

So how was week one? By now you may have undergone a series of attacks by the enemy who does not want you in this program. You may be experiencing everything from being tired and sleepy in the mornings, to procrastination, unbelief in the process, attacks on the job, attacks on your finances, and/or attacks on your family. He will not stop. You cannot stop!

> *Be sober, be vigilant; because your adversary the devil, as [he's not a lion, but he will sure try to make you think he's one] a roaring lion, walketh about, seeking whom he may devour [remember he needs your permission to devour you] (1 Peter 5:8, with my additional comments).*

You've probably never thought about it this way but the enemy brings confirmation. Yep! Hard to imagine but he does. When you're in the right place with God, you're in the Word, praying, studying, checking and your heart posture; the enemy is constantly attacking you. You don't hear from him when you not doing right. At that point, he could care less. You're doing damage to yourself you don't need him.

I won't sugar coat it for you because week two and three will get tougher but so do you. Right now you can't see what's really happening to your heart. During this part of basic training you will be barraged with mental attacks. Remember, you have to have physical and emotional stamina to withstand the enemy's attacks. He will try to break you emotionally.

The routine of the daily exercise are meant to build mental and physical stamina, just like exercising. You are ensuring that your foundation has everything it needs to survive.

Have you been listening to your daily podcast? I cannot be there with you in-person but I'm there with you in spirit. I'm that drill sergeant's voice in your head saying you got this. You can do it. This too shall pass.

Week Two Cadence: "You Can't Break My Spirit"

You can't break my spirit down
You can't break my spirit down

No, you can't break my spirit down
No, you can't break my spirit down

I'm going use The Prayer Box everyday
Use The Prayer Box everyday

Spiritual Discipline the only way
Spiritual Discipline the only way

You can't break my spirit down
You can't break my spirit down

No, you can't break my spirit down
No, you can't break my spirit down

"You can't Break My Body Down" is a military cadence. No information on author or origin. This cadence has been rewritten by Paula Bryant-Ellis

WEEK TWO - DAY EIGHT

Start Time: _____ **AM/PM**

Did you add your appointment with the Holy Spirit to your daily calendar? Make it a recurring appointment with no ending date.

How long did you pray: _____ **MINUTES/HOURS**

Start with a minimum of 15-20 minutes, and work your way up from there by adding 5-10 minutes each week. I want you to get in the habit of spending time with the Holy Spirit. Show up on time and be consistent. Just like with any relationship, the more time you spend together, the more intimacy and trust you have in the relationship.

Did you take your communion for the week? YES / NO

What's your reason for taking communion this week? What are you asking the Holy Spirit to do or to change in your life?

_____

_____

What scripture(s) did you select for the week?

What spiritual warfare are you in right now; battling the mind and being focused, taking communion (make sure your heart posture is pure), needing influence and favor, consistent prayer life, humility in your praise, complete surrender in reverence and worship?

Scripture #1

_____

_____

_____

_____

Scripture #2

_____

_____

_____

Always start your prayer time with praise and worship (you don't always have to use music for praise and worship). **What song did you select today, if any?**

_____

_____

_____

Was there anything in particular that you needed from the song you selected? When I'm in a dry place or in a deep battle, I need music to help me start my mornings. But you will get to a place that you won't need music to help you enter into His Presence. Once you start spending quality time together, you just enter in and start praising Him and the tears will begin to flow.

_____

_____

_____

_____

What did you pray about today (make sure to write it in **BLACK** ink)? **What direction or revelation did the Holy Spirit give you today?** Start dedicating at least 10 minutes after prayer to just sit in complete quietness and listen to the Voice of the Holy Spirit (make sure to write it in **RED** ink). **Were you able to release anything that was hindering you from spending time in the Presence of God?**

_____

_____

WEEK TWO - DAY NINE

Start Time: _____ **AM/PM**

Did you add your appointment with the Holy Spirit to your daily calendar? Make it a recurring appointment with no ending date.

How long did you pray: _____ **MINUTES/HOURS**

Start with a minimum of 15-20 minutes, and work your way up from there by adding 5-10 minutes each week. I want you to get in the habit of spending time with the Holy Spirit. Show up on time and be consistent. Just like with any relationship, the more time you spend together, the more intimacy and trust you have in the relationship.

What scripture(s) did you select for the week?

What spiritual warfare are you in right now; battling the mind and being focused, taking communion (make sure your heart posture is pure), needing influence and favor, consistent prayer life, humility in your praise, complete surrender in reverence and worship?

Scripture #1

_____

_____

_____

Scripture #2

_____

_____

_____

_____

Always start your prayer time with praise and worship (you don't always have to use music for praise and worship). **What song did you select today, if any?**

_____

_____

Was there anything in particular that you needed from the song you selected? When I'm in a dry place or in a deep battle, I need music to help me start my mornings. But you will get to a place that you won't need music to help you enter into His Presence. Once you start spending quality time together, you just enter in and start praising Him and the tears will begin to flow.

_____

_____

_____

What did you pray about today (make sure to write it in **BLACK** ink)? **What direction or revelation did the Holy Spirit give you today?** Start dedicating at least 10 minutes after prayer to just sit in complete quietness and listen to the Voice of the Holy Spirit (make sure to write it in **RED** ink). **Were you able to release anything that was hindering you from spending time in the Presence of God?**

_____

_____

_____

_____

_____

_____

WEEK TWO - DAY TEN

Start Time: _____ **AM/PM**

Did you add your appointment with the Holy Spirit to your daily calendar? Make it a recurring appointment with no ending date.

How long did you pray: _____ **MINUTES/HOURS**

Start with a minimum of 15-20 minutes, and work your way up from there by adding 5-10 minutes each week. I want you to get in the habit of spending time with the Holy Spirit. Show up on time and be consistent. Just like with any relationship, the more time you spend together, the more intimacy and trust you have in the relationship.

What scripture(s) did you select for the week?

What spiritual warfare are you in right now; battling the mind and being focused, taking communion (make sure your heart posture is pure), needing influence and favor, consistent prayer life, humility in your praise, complete surrender in reverence and worship?

Scripture #1

_____

_____

_____

Scripture #2

_____

_____

_____

_____

Always start your prayer time with praise and worship (you don't always have to use music for praise and worship). **What song did you select today, if any?**

_____

_____

Was there anything in particular that you needed from the song you selected? When I'm in a dry place or in a deep battle, I need music to help me start my mornings. But you will get to a place that you won't need music to help you enter into His Presence. Once you start spending quality time together, you just enter in and start praising Him and the tears will begin to flow.

_____

_____

_____

_____

What did you pray about today (make sure to write it in **BLACK** ink)? **What direction or revelation did the Holy Spirit give you today?** Start dedicating at least 10 minutes after prayer to just sit in complete quietness and listen to the Voice of the Holy Spirit (make sure to write it in **RED** ink). **Were you able to release anything that was hindering you from spending time in the Presence of God?**

_____

_____

_____

_____

_____

_____

WEEK TWO - DAY ELEVEN

Start Time: _____ **AM/PM**

Did you add your appointment with the Holy Spirit to your daily calendar? Make it a recurring appointment with no ending date.

How long did you pray: _____ **MINUTES/HOURS**

Start with a minimum of 15-20 minutes, and work your way up from there by adding 5-10 minutes each week. I want you to get in the habit of spending time with the Holy Spirit. Show up on time and be consistent. Just like with any relationship, the more time you spend together, the more intimacy and trust you have in the relationship.

What scripture(s) did you select for the week?

What spiritual warfare are you in right now; battling the mind and being focused, taking communion (make sure your heart posture is pure), needing influence and favor, consistent prayer life, humility in your praise, complete surrender in reverence and worship?

Scripture #1

_____

_____

_____

Scripture #2

_____

_____

_____

_____

Always start your prayer time with praise and worship (you don't always have to use music for praise and worship). **What song did you select today, if any?**

_____

_____

Was there anything in particular that you needed from the song you selected? When I'm in a dry place or in a deep battle, I need music to help me start my mornings. But you will get to a place that you won't need music to help you enter into His Presence. Once you start spending quality time together, you just enter in and start praising Him and the tears will begin to flow.

_____

_____

_____

_____

What did you pray about today (make sure to write it in **BLACK** ink)**? What direction or revelation did the Holy Spirit give you today?** Start dedicating at least 10 minutes after prayer to just sit in complete quietness and listen to the Voice of the Holy Spirit (make sure to write it in **RED** ink). **Were you able to release anything that was hindering you from spending time in the Presence of God?**

_____

_____

_____

_____

_____

_____

WEEK TWO - DAY TWELVE

Start Time: _____ **AM/PM**

Did you add your appointment with the Holy Spirit to your daily calendar? Make it a recurring appointment with no ending date.

How long did you pray: _____ **MINUTES/HOURS**

Start with a minimum of 15-20 minutes, and work your way up from there by adding 5-10 minutes each week. I want you to get in the habit of spending time with the Holy Spirit. Show up on time and be consistent. Just like with any relationship, the more time you spend together, the more intimacy and trust you have in the relationship.

What scripture(s) did you select for the week?

What spiritual warfare are you in right now; battling the mind and being focused, taking communion (make sure your heart posture is pure), needing influence and favor, consistent prayer life, humility in your praise, complete surrender in reverence and worship?

Scripture #1

_____

_____

_____

Scripture #2

_____

_____

_____

Always start your prayer time with praise and worship (you don't always have to use music for praise and worship). **What song did you select today, if any?**

_____

_____

Was there anything in particular that you needed from the song you selected? When I'm in a dry place or in a deep battle, I need music to help me start my mornings. But you will get to a place that you won't need music to help you enter into His Presence. Once you start spending quality time together, you just enter in and start praising Him and the tears will begin to flow.

_____

_____

_____

_____

What did you pray about today (make sure to write it in **BLACK** ink)**? What direction or revelation did the Holy Spirit give you today?** Start dedicating at least 10 minutes after prayer to just sit in complete quietness and listen to the Voice of the Holy Spirit (make sure to write it in **RED** ink). **Were you able to release anything that was hindering you from spending time in the Presence of God?**

_____

_____

_____

_____

_____

_____

WEEK TWO - DAY THIRTEEN

Start Time: _____ **AM/PM**

Did you add your appointment with the Holy Spirit to your daily calendar? Make it a recurring appointment with no ending date.

How long did you pray: _____ **MINUTES/HOURS**

Start with a minimum of 15-20 minutes, and work your way up from there by adding 5-10 minutes each week. I want you to get in the habit of spending time with the Holy Spirit. Show up on time and be consistent. Just like with any relationship, the more time you spend together, the more intimacy and trust you have in the relationship.

What scripture(s) did you select for the week?

What spiritual warfare are you in right now; battling the mind and being focused, taking communion (make sure your heart posture is pure), needing influence and favor, consistent prayer life, humility in your praise, complete surrender in reverence and worship?

Scripture #1

_____

_____

_____

Scripture #2

_____

_____

_____

Always start your prayer time with praise and worship (you don't always have to use music for praise and worship). **What song did you select today, if any?**

_____

_____

Was there anything in particular that you needed from the song you selected? When I'm in a dry place or in a deep battle, I need music to help me start my mornings. But you will get to a place that you won't need music to help you enter into His Presence. Once you start spending quality time together, you just enter in and start praising Him and the tears will begin to flow.

_____

_____

_____

_____

What did you pray about today (make sure to write it in **BLACK** ink)**? What direction or revelation did the Holy Spirit give you today?** Start dedicating at least 10 minutes after prayer to just sit in complete quietness and listen to the Voice of the Holy Spirit (make sure to write it in **RED** ink). **Were you able to release anything that was hindering you from spending time in the Presence of God?**

_____

_____

_____

_____

_____

_____

WEEK TWO - DAY FOURTEEN

Start Time: _____ **AM/PM**

Did you add your appointment with the Holy Spirit to your daily calendar? Make it a recurring appointment with no ending date.

How long did you pray: _____ **MINUTES/HOURS**

Start with a minimum of 15-20 minutes, and work your way up from there by adding 5-10 minutes each week. I want you to get in the habit of spending time with the Holy Spirit. Show up on time and be consistent. Just like with any relationship, the more time you spend together, the more intimacy and trust you have in the relationship.

What scripture(s) did you select for the week?

What spiritual warfare are you in right now; battling the mind and being focused, taking communion (make sure your heart posture is pure), needing influence and favor, consistent prayer life, humility in your praise, complete surrender in reverence and worship?

Scripture #1

_____

_____

_____

Scripture #2

_____

_____

_____

_____

Always start your prayer time with praise and worship (you don't always have to use music for praise and worship). **What song did you select today, if any?**

_____

_____

Was there anything in particular that you needed from the song you selected? When I'm in a dry place or in a deep battle, I need music to help me start my mornings. But you will get to a place that you won't need music to help you enter into His Presence. Once you start spending quality time together, you just enter in and start praising Him and the tears will begin to flow.

_____

_____

_____

_____

What did you pray about today (make sure to write it in **BLACK** ink)? **What direction or revelation did the Holy Spirit give you today?** Start dedicating at least 10 minutes after prayer to just sit in complete quietness and listen to the Voice of the Holy Spirit (make sure to write it in **RED** ink). **Were you able to release anything that was hindering you from spending time in the Presence of God?**

_____

_____

_____

_____

_____

_____

CHAPTER 8

WEEK THREE ASSIGNMENT

Two weeks under your belt and two weeks to go! I'm so proud of you for staying committed to this journey. I know it can be challenging but you can do it!

Right now pushing through is extremely important. You're in the midst of a mental warfare but you're a fighter! 2 Corinthians 10:5 says,

> *"Casting down imaginations, and every high thing that exalteth itself against the knowledge of God, and bringing into captivity every thought to the obedience of Christ."*

Can you see why having the right scriptures to call on is important? You need to trust and believe what God says about you. The only way to know what He says about you, you have to read the Word of God for yourself.

I know it does not feel like it but you've done a lot in two weeks. I hope you're taking time to study the scriptures and you're looking up every word including their synonyms. You'll learn a lot from this exercise.

I like to compare footings of the foundations to the scriptures because the footings on a building or house go deep. They're set up in their own concrete prior to the entire foundation being poured. They go deep so you can go high. Footings carry the weight of the exterior walls, roof, staircases and beams. Footing placements are strategic.

Scriptures are strategic. That's why it's important to know them and what they mean. Remember, the enemy knows them as well. He once was a beautiful angel and now he's the angry enemy hunting you for your eternity.

As a soldier your muscles should be sore. If they are, that's great! If they're not, it means you're not doing enough heavy lifting or stretching.

Did you sacrifice in the amount of time you set to spend with God? Have you cut back on TV, movies, or other personal activities to spend more time with God? Do you feel the pressure of something slipping or not getting done because you've set aside time to study and pray?

If you're not doing any of these then you're not serious about your relationship. A relationship with God requires sacrifice. There's no other way to do it.

Are you listening to your daily podcast? If so, you know I'm praying for you every day. **DON'T STOP NOW!**

Week Three Cadence: "Mama Mama Can't You See"

Whoa, whoa, whoa, whoa
Whoa, whoa, whoa, whoa

Whoa, whoa, whoa, whoa
Whoa, whoa, whoa, whoa

Whoa, whoa, whoa, whoa
Whoa, whoa, whoa, whoa

Whoa, whoa, whoa, whoa
Whoa, whoa, whoa, whoa

Mama, mama, can't you see
Mama, mama, can't you see

What the Lord has done to me
What the Lord has done to me

Mama, mama, can't you see
Mama, mama, can't you see

What the Lord has done to me
What the Lord has done to me

I use to sleep all day
I use to sleep all day

Now I get up and I pray
Now I get up and I pray

I use to sleep all day
I use to sleep all day

Now I get up and I pray
Now I get up and I pray

Mama don't you cry from me
Mama don't you cry from me

Jesus Christ has set me free
Jesus Christ has set me free.

Whoa, whoa, whoa, whoa
Whoa, whoa, whoa, whoa

Whoa, whoa, whoa, whoa
Whoa, whoa, whoa, whoa

"Mama Mama Can't You See" is a military cadence. No information on author or origin. This cadence has been rewritten by Paula Bryant-Ellis

WEEK THREE - DAY FIFTEEN

Start Time: _____ **AM/PM**

Did you add your appointment with the Holy Spirit to your daily calendar? Make it a recurring appointment with no ending date.

How long did you pray: _____ **MINUTES/HOURS**

Start with a minimum of 15-20 minutes, and work your way up from there by adding 5-10 minutes each week. I want you to get in the habit of spending time with the Holy Spirit. Show up on time and be consistent. Just like with any relationship, the more time you spend together, the more intimacy and trust you have in the relationship.

Did you take your communion for the week? YES / NO

What's your reason for taking communion this week? What are you asking the Holy Spirit to do or to change in your life?

_____

_____

What scripture(s) did you select for the week?

What spiritual warfare are you in right now; battling the mind and being focused, taking communion (make sure your heart posture is pure), needing influence and favor, consistent prayer life, humility in your praise, complete surrender in reverence and worship?

Scripture #1

_____

_____

_____

_____

Scripture #2

_____

_____

Always start your prayer time with praise and worship (you don't always have to use music for praise and worship). **What song did you select today, if any?**

Was there anything in particular that you needed from the song you selected? When I'm in a dry place or in a deep battle, I need music to help me start my mornings. But you will get to a place that you won't need music to help you enter into His Presence. Once you start spending quality time together, you just enter in and start praising Him and the tears will begin to flow.

What did you pray about today (make sure to write it in **BLACK** ink)? **What direction or revelation did the Holy Spirit give you today?** Start dedicating at least 10 minutes after prayer to just sit in complete quietness and listen to the Voice of the Holy Spirit (make sure to write it in **RED** ink). **Were you able to release anything that was hindering you from spending time in the Presence of God?**

WEEK THREE - DAY SIXTEEN

Start Time: _____ **AM/PM**

Did you add your appointment with the Holy Spirit to your daily calendar? Make it a recurring appointment with no ending date.

How long did you pray: _____ **MINUTES/HOURS**

Start with a minimum of 15-20 minutes, and work your way up from there by adding 5-10 minutes each week. I want you to get in the habit of spending time with the Holy Spirit. Show up on time and be consistent. Just like with any relationship, the more time you spend together, the more intimacy and trust you have in the relationship.

What scripture(s) did you select for the week?

What spiritual warfare are you in right now; battling the mind and being focused, taking communion (make sure your heart posture is pure), needing influence and favor, consistent prayer life, humility in your praise, complete surrender in reverence and worship?

Scripture #1

_____

_____

_____

Scripture #2

_____

_____

_____

_____

Always start your prayer time with praise and worship (you don't always have to use music for praise and worship). **What song did you select today, if any?**

_____

_____

Was there anything in particular that you needed from the song you selected? When I'm in a dry place or in a deep battle, I need music to help me start my mornings. But you will get to a place that you won't need music to help you enter into His Presence. Once you start spending quality time together, you just enter in and start praising Him and the tears will begin to flow.

_____

_____

_____

_____

What did you pray about today (make sure to write it in **BLACK** ink)**? What direction or revelation did the Holy Spirit give you today?** Start dedicating at least 10 minutes after prayer to just sit in complete quietness and listen to the Voice of the Holy Spirit (make sure to write it in **RED** ink). **Were you able to release anything that was hindering you from spending time in the Presence of God?**

_____

_____

_____

_____

_____

_____

WEEK THREE - DAY SEVENTEEN

Start Time: _____ **AM/PM**

Did you add your appointment with the Holy Spirit to your daily calendar? Make it a recurring appointment with no ending date.

How long did you pray: _____ **MINUTES/HOURS**

Start with a minimum of 15-20 minutes, and work your way up from there by adding 5-10 minutes each week. I want you to get in the habit of spending time with the Holy Spirit. Show up on time and be consistent. Just like with any relationship, the more time you spend together, the more intimacy and trust you have in the relationship.

What scripture(s) did you select for the week?

What spiritual warfare are you in right now; battling the mind and being focused, taking communion (make sure your heart posture is pure), needing influence and favor, consistent prayer life, humility in your praise, complete surrender in reverence and worship?

Scripture #1

_____

_____

_____

Scripture #2

_____

_____

_____

_____

Always start your prayer time with praise and worship (you don't always have to use music for praise and worship). **What song did you select today, if any?**

_____

_____

Was there anything in particular that you needed from the song you selected? When I'm in a dry place or in a deep battle, I need music to help me start my mornings. But you will get to a place that you won't need music to help you enter into His Presence. Once you start spending quality time together, you just enter in and start praising Him and the tears will begin to flow.

_____

_____

_____

_____

What did you pray about today (make sure to write it in **BLACK** ink)? **What direction or revelation did the Holy Spirit give you today?** Start dedicating at least 10 minutes after prayer to just sit in complete quietness and listen to the Voice of the Holy Spirit (make sure to write it in **RED** ink). **Were you able to release anything that was hindering you from spending time in the Presence of God?**

_____

_____

_____

_____

_____

_____

WEEK THREE - DAY EIGHTEEN

Start Time: _____ **AM/PM**

Did you add your appointment with the Holy Spirit to your daily calendar? Make it a recurring appointment with no ending date.

How long did you pray: _____ **MINUTES/HOURS**

Start with a minimum of 15-20 minutes, and work your way up from there by adding 5-10 minutes each week. I want you to get in the habit of spending time with the Holy Spirit. Show up on time and be consistent. Just like with any relationship, the more time you spend together, the more intimacy and trust you have in the relationship.

What scripture(s) did you select for the week?

What spiritual warfare are you in right now; battling the mind and being focused, taking communion (make sure your heart posture is pure), needing influence and favor, consistent prayer life, humility in your praise, complete surrender in reverence and worship?

Scripture #1

_____

_____

_____

Scripture #2

_____

_____

_____

_____

Always start your prayer time with praise and worship (you don't always have to use music for praise and worship). **What song did you select today, if any?**

_____

_____

Was there anything in particular that you needed from the song you selected? When I'm in a dry place or in a deep battle, I need music to help me start my mornings. But you will get to a place that you won't need music to help you enter into His Presence. Once you start spending quality time together, you just enter in and start praising Him and the tears will begin to flow.

_____

_____

_____

_____

What did you pray about today (make sure to write it in **BLACK** ink)? **What direction or revelation did the Holy Spirit give you today?** Start dedicating at least 10 minutes after prayer to just sit in complete quietness and listen to the Voice of the Holy Spirit (make sure to write it in **RED** ink). **Were you able to release anything that was hindering you from spending time in the Presence of God?**

_____

_____

_____

_____

_____

_____

WEEK THREE - DAY NINETEEN

Start Time: _____ **AM/PM**

Did you add your appointment with the Holy Spirit to your daily calendar? Make it a recurring appointment with no ending date.

How long did you pray: _____ **MINUTES/HOURS**

Start with a minimum of 15-20 minutes, and work your way up from there by adding 5-10 minutes each week. I want you to get in the habit of spending time with the Holy Spirit. Show up on time and be consistent. Just like with any relationship, the more time you spend together, the more intimacy and trust you have in the relationship.

What scripture(s) did you select for the week?

What spiritual warfare are you in right now; battling the mind and being focused, taking communion (make sure your heart posture is pure), needing influence and favor, consistent prayer life, humility in your praise, complete surrender in reverence and worship?

Scripture #1

_____

_____

_____

Scripture #2

_____

_____

_____

_____

_____

Always start your prayer time with praise and worship (you don't always have to use music for praise and worship). **What song did you select today, if any?**

_____

_____

Was there anything in particular that you needed from the song you selected? When I'm in a dry place or in a deep battle, I need music to help me start my mornings. But you will get to a place that you won't need music to help you enter into His Presence. Once you start spending quality time together, you just enter in and start praising Him and the tears will begin to flow.

_____

_____

_____

_____

What did you pray about today (make sure to write it in **BLACK** ink)? **What direction or revelation did the Holy Spirit give you today?** Start dedicating at least 10 minutes after prayer to just sit in complete quietness and listen to the Voice of the Holy Spirit (make sure to write it in **RED** ink). **Were you able to release anything that was hindering you from spending time in the Presence of God?**

_____

_____

_____

_____

_____

_____

WEEK THREE - DAY TWENTY

Start Time: _____ **AM/PM**

Did you add your appointment with the Holy Spirit to your daily calendar? Make it a recurring appointment with no ending date.

How long did you pray: _____ **MINUTES/HOURS**

Start with a minimum of 15-20 minutes, and work your way up from there by adding 5-10 minutes each week. I want you to get in the habit of spending time with the Holy Spirit. Show up on time and be consistent. Just like with any relationship, the more time you spend together, the more intimacy and trust you have in the relationship.

What scripture(s) did you select for the week?

What spiritual warfare are you in right now; battling the mind and being focused, taking communion (make sure your heart posture is pure), needing influence and favor, consistent prayer life, humility in your praise, complete surrender in reverence and worship?

Scripture #1

_____

_____

_____

Scripture #2

_____

_____

_____

_____

Always start your prayer time with praise and worship (you don't always have to use music for praise and worship). **What song did you select today, if any?**

____

____

Was there anything in particular that you needed from the song you selected? When I'm in a dry place or in a deep battle, I need music to help me start my mornings. But you will get to a place that you won't need music to help you enter into His Presence. Once you start spending quality time together, you just enter in and start praising Him and the tears will begin to flow.

____

____

____

____

What did you pray about today (make sure to write it in **BLACK** ink)? **What direction or revelation did the Holy Spirit give you today?** Start dedicating at least 10 minutes after prayer to just sit in complete quietness and listen to the Voice of the Holy Spirit (make sure to write it in **RED** ink). **Were you able to release anything that was hindering you from spending time in the Presence of God?**

____

____

____

____

____

____

____

WEEK THREE - DAY TWENTY ONE

Start Time: _____ **AM/PM**

Did you add your appointment with the Holy Spirit to your daily calendar? Make it a recurring appointment with no ending date.

How long did you pray: _____ **MINUTES/HOURS**

Start with a minimum of 15-20 minutes and work your way up from there by adding 5-10 minutes each week. I want you to get in the habit of spending time with the Holy Spirit. Show up on time and be consistent. Just like with any relationship, the more time you spend together, the more intimacy and trust you have in the relationship.

What scripture(s) did you select for the week?

What spiritual warfare are you in right now; battling the mind and being focused, taking communion (make sure your heart posture is pure), needing influence and favor, consistent prayer life, humility in your praise, complete surrender in reverence and worship?

Scripture #1

_____

_____

_____

Scripture #2

_____

_____

_____

_____

Always start your prayer time with praise and worship (you don't always have to use music for praise and worship). **What song did you select today, if any?**

_____

_____

Was there anything in particular that you needed from the song you selected? When I'm in a dry place or in a deep battle, I need music to help me start my mornings. But you will get to a place that you won't need music to help you enter into His Presence. Once you start spending quality time together, you just enter in and start praising Him and the tears will begin to flow.

_____

_____

_____

_____

What did you pray about today (make sure to write it in **BLACK** ink)? **What direction or revelation did the Holy Spirit give you today?** Start dedicating at least 10 minutes after prayer to just sit in complete quietness and listen to the Voice of the Holy Spirit (make sure to write it in **RED** ink). **Were you able to release anything that was hindering you from spending time in the Presence of God?**

_____

_____

_____

_____

_____

_____

CHAPTER 9

WEEK FOUR ASSIGNMENT

Can you believe you are about to start week four? You've been consistently and diligently on your knees in private communications with the Holy Spirit! How can something so beautiful be so challenging?

You have something inside of you that was made exclusively for the Kingdom. You my friend were born with a gift but your purpose now that's given. Your advisory does not want the two together. Sure you can tap into your gift. We see people do it all the time. They're not serving the Kingdom but yet they've found a way to tap into their gift. On the outside it looks as though it's sustaining them. But on the inside they've sold their soul to another spirit and it's not the Holy Spirit.

Your gift has a mate and its name is purpose. You can only find your purpose when you align with the Kingdom. God will never allow you to use the purpose He's given you for anything else. Your gift yes, His purpose, no!

If you were in high school this would be your senior year. Remember how difficult it was to find your way? At least it was for me. But four years later, it was your turn to walk down that aisle and get that diploma and not a moment too soon. You couldn't pay me enough to go back to that again.

Well, that's what it's like if you stop. Who wants to start as a freshman again?

There's another week of podcast so don't forget to check them out. Just seven days away. You're a senior now!

<u>Week Four Cadence:</u> "They Say That In The Kingdom"

They say that in the Kingdom
They say that in the Kingdom

The streets are paved with gold
The streets are paved with gold

One day I'm going to see it
One day I'm going to see it

I'm going to make it home
I'm going to make it home

They say that in the Kingdom
They say that in the Kingdom

The angels sing His praise
The angels sing His praise

The Alpha and Omega
The Alpha and Omega

Jehovah is His Name
Jehovah is His Name

"They Say That In The Navy" is a military cadence. No information on author or origin. This cadence has been rewritten by Paula Bryant-Ellis

WEEK FOUR - DAY TWENTY TWO

Start Time: _____ **AM/PM**

Did you add your appointment with the Holy Spirit to your daily calendar? Make it a recurring appointment with no ending date.

How long did you pray: _____ **MINUTES/HOURS**

Start with a minimum of 15-20 minutes and work your way up from there by adding 5-10 minutes each week. I want you to get in the habit of spending time with the Holy Spirit. Show up on time and be consistent. Just like with any relationship, the more time you spend together, the more intimacy and trust you have in the relationship.

Did you take your communion for the week? YES / NO

What's your reason for taking communion this week? What are you asking the Holy Spirit to do or to change in your life?

_____

_____

_____

_____

What scripture(s) did you select for the week?

What spiritual warfare are you in right now; battling the mind and being focused, taking communion (make sure your heart posture is pure), needing influence and favor, consistent prayer life, humility in your praise, complete surrender in reverence and worship?

Scripture #1

_____

_____

Scripture #2

_____

_____

Always start your prayer time with praise and worship (you don't always have to use music for praise and worship). **What song did you select today, if any?**

_____

_____

Was there anything in particular that you needed from the song you selected? When I'm in a dry place or in a deep battle, I need music to help me start my mornings. But you will get to a place that you won't need music to help you enter into His Presence. Once you start spending quality time together, you just enter in and start praising Him and the tears will begin to flow.

_____

_____

_____

What did you pray about today (make sure to write it in **BLACK** ink)**? What direction or revelation did the Holy Spirit give you today?** Start dedicating at least 10 minutes after prayer to just sit in complete quietness and listen to the Voice of the Holy Spirit (make sure to write it in **RED** ink). **Were you able to release anything that was hindering you from spending time in the Presence of God?**

_____

_____

_____

_____

_____

_____

WEEK FOUR - DAY TWENTY THREE

Start Time: _____   **AM/PM**

Did you add your appointment with the Holy Spirit to your daily calendar? Make it a recurring appointment with no ending date.

How long did you pray: _____   **MINUTES/HOURS**

Start with a minimum of 15-20 minutes and work your way up from there by adding 5-10 minutes each week. I want you to get in the habit of spending time with the Holy Spirit. Show up on time and be consistent. Just like with any relationship, the more time you spend together, the more intimacy and trust you have in the relationship.

What scripture(s) did you select for the week?

What spiritual warfare are you in right now; battling the mind and being focused, taking communion (make sure your heart posture is pure), needing influence and favor, consistent prayer life, humility in your praise, complete surrender in reverence and worship?

Scripture #1

_____

_____

_____

Scripture #2

_____

_____

_____

Always start your prayer time with praise and worship (you don't always have to use music for praise and worship). **What song did you select today, if any?**

_____

_____

Was there anything in particular that you needed from the song you selected? When I'm in a dry place or in a deep battle, I need music to help me start my mornings. But you will get to a place that you won't need music to help you enter into His Presence. Once you start spending quality time together, you just enter in and start praising Him and the tears will begin to flow.

_____

_____

_____

What did you pray about today (make sure to write it in **BLACK** ink)? **What direction or revelation did the Holy Spirit give you today?** Start dedicating at least 10 minutes after prayer to just sit in complete quietness and listen to the Voice of the Holy Spirit (make sure to write it in **RED** ink). **Were you able to release anything that was hindering you from spending time in the Presence of God?**

_____

_____

_____

_____

_____

_____

WEEK FOUR - DAY TWENTY FOUR

Start Time: _____ **AM/PM**

Did you add your appointment with the Holy Spirit to your daily calendar? Make it a recurring appointment with no ending date.

How long did you pray: _____ **MINUTES/HOURS**

Start with a minimum of 15-20 minutes and work your way up from there by adding 5-10 minutes each week. I want you to get in the habit of spending time with the Holy Spirit. Show up on time and be consistent. Just like with any relationship, the more time you spend together, the more intimacy and trust you have in the relationship.

What scripture(s) did you select for the week?

What spiritual warfare are you in right now; battling the mind and being focused, taking communion (make sure your heart posture is pure), needing influence and favor, consistent prayer life, humility in your praise, complete surrender in reverence and worship?

Scripture #1

_____

_____

_____

Scripture #2

_____

_____

_____

_____

Always start your prayer time with praise and worship (you don't always have to use music for praise and worship). **What song did you select today, if any?**

_____

_____

Was there anything in particular that you needed from the song you selected? When I'm in a dry place or in a deep battle, I need music to help me start my mornings. But you will get to a place that you won't need music to help you enter into His Presence. Once you start spending quality time together, you just enter in and start praising Him and the tears will begin to flow.

_____

_____

_____

_____

What did you pray about today (make sure to write it in **BLACK** ink)? **What direction or revelation did the Holy Spirit give you today?** Start dedicating at least 10 minutes after prayer to just sit in complete quietness and listen to the Voice of the Holy Spirit (make sure to write it in **RED** ink). **Were you able to release anything that was hindering you from spending time in the Presence of God?**

_____

_____

_____

_____

_____

_____

WEEK FOUR - DAY TWENTY FIVE

Start Time: _____ **AM/PM**

Did you add your appointment with the Holy Spirit to your daily calendar? Make it a recurring appointment with no ending date.

How long did you pray: _____ **MINUTES/HOURS**

Start with a minimum of 15-20 minutes and work your way up from there by adding 5-10 minutes each week. I want you to get in the habit of spending time with the Holy Spirit. Show up on time and be consistent. Just like with any relationship, the more time you spend together, the more intimacy and trust you have in the relationship.

What scripture(s) did you select for the week?

What spiritual warfare are you in right now; battling the mind and being focused, taking communion (make sure your heart posture is pure), needing influence and favor, consistent prayer life, humility in your praise, complete surrender in reverence and worship?

Scripture #1

_____

_____

_____

Scripture #2

_____

_____

_____

_____

_____

Always start your prayer time with praise and worship (you don't always have to use music for praise and worship). **What song did you select today, if any?**

_____

_____

Was there anything in particular that you needed from the song you selected? When I'm in a dry place or in a deep battle, I need music to help me start my mornings. But you will get to a place that you won't need music to help you enter into His Presence. Once you start spending quality time together, you just enter in and start praising Him and the tears will begin to flow.

_____

_____

_____

_____

What did you pray about today (make sure to write it in **BLACK** ink)**? What direction or revelation did the Holy Spirit give you today?** Start dedicating at least 10 minutes after prayer to just sit in complete quietness and listen to the Voice of the Holy Spirit (make sure to write it in **RED** ink). **Were you able to release anything that was hindering you from spending time in the Presence of God?**

_____

_____

_____

_____

_____

_____

_____

WEEK FOUR - DAY TWENTY SIX

Start Time: _____ **AM/PM**

Did you add your appointment with the Holy Spirit to your daily calendar? Make it a recurring appointment with no ending date.

How long did you pray: _____ **MINUTES/HOURS**

Start with a minimum of 15-20 minutes and work your way up from there by adding 5-10 minutes each week. I want you to get in the habit of spending time with the Holy Spirit. Show up on time and be consistent. Just like with any relationship, the more time you spend together, the more intimacy and trust you have in the relationship.

What scripture(s) did you select for the week?

What spiritual warfare are you in right now; battling the mind and being focused, taking communion (make sure your heart posture is pure), needing influence and favor, consistent prayer life, humility in your praise, complete surrender in reverence and worship?

Scripture #1

_____

_____

_____

Scripture #2

_____

_____

_____

_____

Always start your prayer time with praise and worship (you don't always have to use music for praise and worship). **What song did you select today, if any?**

_____

_____

Was there anything in particular that you needed from the song you selected? When I'm in a dry place or in a deep battle, I need music to help me start my mornings. But you will get to a place that you won't need music to help you enter into His Presence. Once you start spending quality time together, you just enter in and start praising Him and the tears will begin to flow.

_____

_____

_____

_____

What did you pray about today (make sure to write it in **BLACK** ink)**? What direction or revelation did the Holy Spirit give you today?** Start dedicating at least 10 minutes after prayer to just sit in complete quietness and listen to the Voice of the Holy Spirit (make sure to write it in **RED** ink). **Were you able to release anything that was hindering you from spending time in the Presence of God?**

_____

_____

_____

_____

_____

_____

WEEK FOUR - DAY TWENTY SEVEN

Start Time: _____ **AM/PM**

Did you add your appointment with the Holy Spirit to your daily calendar? Make it a recurring appointment with no ending date.

How long did you pray: _____ **MINUTES/HOURS**

Start with a minimum of 15-20 minutes and work your way up from there by adding 5-10 minutes each week. I want you to get in the habit of spending time with the Holy Spirit. Show up on time and be consistent. Just like with any relationship, the more time you spend together, the more intimacy and trust you have in the relationship.

What scripture(s) did you select for the week?

What spiritual warfare are you in right now; battling the mind and being focused, taking communion (make sure your heart posture is pure), needing influence and favor, consistent prayer life, humility in your praise, complete surrender in reverence and worship?

Scripture #1

_____

_____

_____

Scripture #2

_____

_____

_____

_____

Always start your prayer time with praise and worship (you don't always have to use music for praise and worship). **What song did you select today, if any?**

_____

_____

Was there anything in particular that you needed from the song you selected? When I'm in a dry place or in a deep battle, I need music to help me start my mornings. But you will get to a place that you won't need music to help you enter into His Presence. Once you start spending quality time together, you just enter in and start praising Him and the tears will begin to flow.

_____

_____

_____

_____

What did you pray about today (make sure to write it in **BLACK** ink)? **What direction or revelation did the Holy Spirit give you today?** Start dedicating at least 10 minutes after prayer to just sit in complete quietness and listen to the Voice of the Holy Spirit (make sure to write it in **RED** ink). **Were you able to release anything that was hindering you from spending time in the Presence of God?**

_____

_____

_____

_____

_____

_____

WEEK FOUR - DAY TWENTY EIGHT

Start Time: _____ **AM/PM**

Did you add your appointment with the Holy Spirit to your daily calendar? Make it a recurring appointment with no ending date.

How long did you pray: _____ **MINUTES/HOURS**

Start with a minimum of 15-20 minutes and work your way up from there by adding 5-10 minutes each week. I want you to get in the habit of spending time with the Holy Spirit. Show up on time and be consistent. Just like with any relationship, the more time you spend together, the more intimacy and trust you have in the relationship.

What scripture(s) did you select for the week?

What spiritual warfare are you in right now; battling the mind and being focused, taking communion (make sure your heart posture is pure), needing influence and favor, consistent prayer life, humility in your praise, complete surrender in reverence and worship?

Scripture #1

_____

_____

_____

Scripture #2

_____

_____

_____

_____

Always start your prayer time with praise and worship (you don't always have to use music for praise and worship). **What song did you select today, if any?**

_____

_____

Was there anything in particular that you needed from the song you selected? When I'm in a dry place or in a deep battle, I need music to help me start my mornings. But you will get to a place that you won't need music to help you enter into His Presence. Once you start spending quality time together, you just enter in and start praising Him and the tears will begin to flow.

_____

_____

_____

_____

What did you pray about today (make sure to write it in **BLACK** ink)**? What direction or revelation did the Holy Spirit give you today?** Start dedicating at least 10 minutes after prayer to just sit in complete quietness and listen to the Voice of the Holy Spirit (make sure to write it in **RED** ink). **Were you able to release anything that was hindering you from spending time in the Presence of God?**

_____

_____

_____

_____

_____

_____

WEEK FOUR - DAY TWENTY NINE

Start Time: _____ **AM/PM**

Did you add your appointment with the Holy Spirit to your daily calendar? Make it a recurring appointment with no ending date.

How long did you pray: _____ **MINUTES/HOURS**

Start with a minimum of 15-20 minutes and work your way up from there by adding 5-10 minutes each week. I want you to get in the habit of spending time with the Holy Spirit. Show up on time and be consistent. Just like with any relationship, the more time you spend together, the more intimacy and trust you have in the relationship.

What scripture(s) did you select for the week?

What spiritual warfare are you in right now; battling the mind and being focused, taking communion (make sure your heart posture is pure), needing influence and favor, consistent prayer life, humility in your praise, complete surrender in reverence and worship?

Scripture #1

_____

_____

_____

Scripture #2

_____

_____

_____

_____

Always start your prayer time with praise and worship (you don't always have to use music for praise and worship). **What song did you select today, if any?**

_____

_____

Was there anything in particular that you needed from the song you selected? When I'm in a dry place or in a deep battle, I need music to help me start my mornings. But you will get to a place that you won't need music to help you enter into His Presence. Once you start spending quality time together, you just enter in and start praising Him and the tears will begin to flow.

_____

_____

_____

_____

What did you pray about today (make sure to write it in **BLACK** ink)? **What direction or revelation did the Holy Spirit give you today?** Start dedicating at least 10 minutes after prayer to just sit in complete quietness and listen to the Voice of the Holy Spirit (make sure to write it in **RED** ink). **Were you able to release anything that was hindering you from spending time in the Presence of God?**

_____

_____

_____

_____

_____

_____

_____

WEEK FOUR - DAY THIRTY

Start Time: _____ **AM/PM**

Did you add your appointment with the Holy Spirit to your daily calendar? Make it a recurring appointment with no ending date.

How long did you pray: _____ **MINUTES/HOURS**

Start with a minimum of 15-20 minutes and work your way up from there by adding 5-10 minutes each week. I want you to get in the habit of spending time with the Holy Spirit. Show up on time and be consistent. Just like with any relationship, the more time you spend together, the more intimacy and trust you have in the relationship.

What scripture(s) did you select for the week?

What spiritual warfare are you in right now; battling the mind and being focused, taking communion (make sure your heart posture is pure), needing influence and favor, consistent prayer life, humility in your praise, complete surrender in reverence and worship?

Scripture #1

_____

_____

_____

Scripture #2

_____

_____

_____

_____

Always start your prayer time with praise and worship (you don't always have to use music for praise and worship). **What song did you select today, if any?**

_____

_____

Was there anything in particular that you needed from the song you selected? When I'm in a dry place or in a deep battle, I need music to help me start my mornings. But you will get to a place that you won't need music to help you enter into His Presence. Once you start spending quality time together, you just enter in and start praising Him and the tears will begin to flow.

_____

_____

_____

_____

What did you pray about today (make sure to write it in **BLACK** ink)**? What direction or revelation did the Holy Spirit give you today?** Start dedicating at least 10 minutes after prayer to just sit in complete quietness and listen to the Voice of the Holy Spirit (make sure to write it in **RED** ink). **Were you able to release anything that was hindering you from spending time in the Presence of God?**

_____

_____

_____

_____

_____

_____

_____

THERE'S POWER IN HABIT

You did it! I hope you better understand the importance of developing good, consistent prayer habits. This is a new beginning! The power in your prayers will increase when you show up time and time again.

Think about any job you've ever had or any class you've ever taken in school. When you started, you didn't know everything you needed to know. You had to learn about the company, department, assignment or task at hand. But YOU SHOWED UP and you kept showing up until one day without even thinking about it you were doing it. Good prayer habits are just like good work habits. THERE'S POWER IN HABIT.

Prayer is God's idea. Prayer is access to God. Prayer is not optional. God wants to talk to you! But you must show up, and you must be consistent. I'm not talking about following some mundane routine. I'm talking about showing up with expectation. Enter into His gates with thanksgiving. Enter into His courts with praise. When you do He won't disappoint you I promise. When you pray to the Father, don't worry about anything other than bringing your own personal aroma of prayer.

Spending time with God is like watching interest grow on your savings account. As a banker in my previous life, I was always surprised to see how many people did not have a savings account or put away a couple of dollars each month for an emergency fund. Saving is a form of discipline, like praying. I've seen people making minimum wage save unbelievable amounts of money. How? Discipline. It's been proven time and time again, that the amount of money you earn has nothing to do with saving money. It's your priorities. It is the same with prayer.

When my husband and I first were first married, we were struggling financially. I was 19 years old and he was 18 years old. We had a child on the way, I didn't work and we lived over 3,000 miles from both our parents.

We were not disciplined savers but I knew we had to have something put away for a rainy day. We were going to need it as young parents. We lived in South Carolina at the time and my mother lived in California. I opened an account at a bank that was only in California. I added my mom to the account in case of an emergency. Then each month, I would mail ten, twenty dollars; whatever we had to the account. It wasn't much but it adds up. When that rainy day came-a-calling (and it did) we'd saved a little nest egg. If you don't deposit anything, it can never earn any interest. Get it? That's what it's like when you do not pray. There's nothing to draw on principal or interest.

I'm so excited that you've spent the last 30 days making daily deposits into your Kingdom account. Keep it up! Never stop! Remember, prayer is not optional. If you're not willing to make a deposit, you shouldn't expect a return.

You're a soldier now! This is the beginning of a whole new prayer life. Don't let me make you think it easy from here. In fact remember what I told you earlier? Attacks, challenges, hurdles are confirmation you're in the right place. Learn to celebrate in the midst of your tears. That's what I've learned to do.

This assignment, to create this box, was not easy. Trust me I've had my share of attacks and have cried a lot of tears to bring this box to fruition. My prayer life has been under constant attack. The very thing I'm writing to you about is what's been the toughest for me over the last 6 months. A couple of weeks ago, I just sat in my prayer corner and cried. Afterwards, I got up and I keep fighting!

I'm going to leave you with this scripture.

> *If my people, which are called by my name, shall humble themselves, and pray, and seek my face, and turn from their wicked ways; then will I hear from heaven, and will forgive their sin, and will heal their land (2 Chronicles 7:14).*

Remember, THERE'S POWER IN HABIT.

ABOUT THE AUTHOR

Paula Bryant-Ellis is a Los Angeles-based film director and producer. Prior to returning to the entertainment industry, where she started her career as an accountant in television, she held multiple leadership roles in banking and finance; including Chief Operating Officer.

She studied filmmaking and producing at the New York Film Academy in New York and Los Angeles. She's a graduate of Massachusetts Institute of Technology (MIT) Sloan School of Management. She holds an MBA from the University of Phoenix and a BA in Accounting from the Concordia University.

She's a wife (married 37 years), mother and entrepreneur. She understands the challenges women face today with relationships, families and careers.

Through her blog, MARY ESTHER RUTH she shares inspirational stories about her life and relationship with Christ.

To find out more about MARY ESTHER RUTH, please visit **maryestherruth.com**

To find out more about Paula Bryant-Ellis and her journey as a new film director and producer, please visit: **paulabryant-ellis.com**

Made in the USA
Middletown, DE
06 May 2019